MYSTERIES
OF HISTORY
IN SUSSEX

Philip Pavey

Front cover and maps © Louis Mackay
www.louismackaydesign.co.uk

Published by Pomegranate Press,
Dolphin House, 51 St Nicholas Lane, Lewes, Sussex BN7 2JZ
pomegranatepress@aol.com
www.pomegranate-press.co.uk

ISBN: 978–1–907242–31–1

British Library Cataloguing-in-Publication Data.
A catalogue record for this book is available from the British Library

Printed and bound by 4Edge, 7A Eldon Way, Hockley, Essex SS5 4AD

CONTENTS

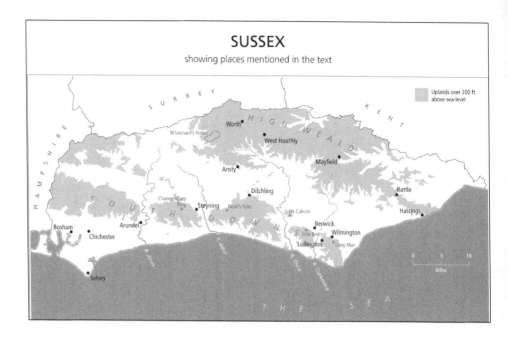

SUSSEX

showing places mentioned in the text

Uplands over 200 ft above sea-level

ABOUT THE AUTHOR

Philip Pavey was born and brought up in Brighton, with family roots in Falmer, Burgess Hill and Slinfold. He has always loved country walking, particularly in Sussex, and studying history, and in this book he brings together these two passions.

His aim has been to combine a methodical approach to history with an accessible style to explore some fascinating mysteries in the past of this beautiful county.

INTRODUCTION

Sussex, for those without the good fortune to know it, is one of the forty traditional counties or primary administrative units of England. It lies along the south-east coast, being about eighty miles long from east to west, and its inland boundary is a shallow arc about 25 miles from north to south at its maximum. Its natural north-western to north-eastern boundary was a thick forest known to the Anglo-Saxons as Andreadesweald, and parts of this still survive in St. Leonard's, Tilgate, Worth, Balcombe and Ashdown forests. On the far west it is bounded by the low lying wetlands around Chichester Harbour, and in the far east by Romney Marsh.

Its neighbouring counties are Hampshire to the west, Surrey to the north-west and north and Kent to the north-east and east. Beyond Surrey is London, which is about 25 miles north of Sussex's northernmost place, Gatwick (which is of course home to the capital's second airport), and 52 miles north of its biggest town, Brighton, with which it has a fast rail link and many cultural and historical ties. The southern coast of the county, along the English Channel, has a similar long-standing relationship with the opposite northern coast of France, Brighton being twinned with the Normandy town of Dieppe which lies only 68 miles distant, and which is linked by ferry from Brighton's neighbour Newhaven.

Topographically, Sussex comprises four east-west bands determined by geology. Along the coast from Chichester to Seaford is a narrow alluvial strip now almost entirely occupied by urban development – seaside towns with only a few gaps, mostly where south-flowing rivers (the Arun, Adur, Ouse and Cuckmere) enter the sea. North of this lie the South Downs, a range of rounded chalk hills with rural villages along their spring line and river valleys, of such beauty that the area was in 2010 designated England's tenth national park. The hills dramatically reach the sea as the cliffs at Beachy Head. North of the Downs lies the Low Weald, a patchwork quilt of farms, fields, lanes and woods which typify what many people picture as the English countryside. This area reaches the sea east of Beachy Head, from where it forms a low lying coastline from Eastbourne via Pevensey to Hastings and Rye – for centuries an inviting landfall for would-be invaders. North of this band is the High Weald, an elevated woodland area which runs along the north of the county and eastwards into Kent.

While these bands determine changes of scenery as the traveller proceeds north or south, some people also detect subtle differences of culture between west and east. The west can seem to have a touch of the atmosphere of land still further west, successively Celtic, Catholic and Royalist. The east, with its generally lower and more open terrain can feel more akin to Kent, Essex and Anglia, successively Germanic, Protestant and Parliamentarian. But too much should not be made of this. The division in 1888 into two administrative counties, East and West Sussex, was necessitated solely by population growth and, despite becoming 'ceremonial counties' more recently, the two areas do not inspire partisan feelings or competing loyalties.

The creation of Brighton and Hove City Council in 2000 means there are now three separate primary local authorities within the historic county, but there is still much to bind the three together. Shared institutions as diverse as Sussex Police, BBC Radio Sussex, Sussex County Cricket Club, the University of Sussex, Harvey's Sussex Ales and the Church of England diocese of Chichester (as ever, coterminous with the county) are underpinned by a strong sense of unique identity stretching far back into history. Some of the intriguing unanswered questions of that history are the subject of this book.

Philip Pavey
2012

1 WHEN DID SUSSEX START?

It is a mystery when Sussex, or the area broadly within its boundaries, came into existence as an administrative or governmental unit. The name is derived from *Su Seaxe*, which is Anglo-Saxon for 'South Saxons', and some evidence points to a foundation in the early Anglo-Saxon period, ie in the fifth century. The Byzantine historian Zosimus, writing around the year 500, says that in 409, after a withdrawal of Roman troops from the defence of Britain against barbarian attacks to fight elsewhere, the Britons "revolted from the Roman empire, no longer submitted to Roman law, and reverted to their native customs..... expelling the Roman magistrates and establishing the government they wanted" [1]. Either in response to a change of heart by the Britons, or to put a brave face on things, the Roman emperor Honorius "sent letters to the cities in Britain urging them to fend for themselves" [2].

Another and contemporary Byzantine historian, Procopius, adds that "the Romans were no longer able to recover Britain, which from that time on continued to be ruled by tyrants" (ie unauthorised rulers, not necessarily despots) [3]. So the Romans never returned, and Britain's Romano-Celtic people were left with the responsibility for defending themselves against the Irish, Pictish and Germanic raiders assailing their shores. It appears they had a tough time of it. Writing in mid-century, St Patrick recounted his kidnap from coastal northern Britain by pirates and his enslavement in Ireland in his youth [4], which is likely to have been around the time the Romans left.

When Bishop Germanus of Auxerre visited twenty years later, in 429, he was greeted by the richly arrayed town dignitaries of Verulamium (St Albans) while visiting the shrine of Britain's first Christian martyr. However, the countryside outside the city was being ravaged by a war band of Picts and Saxons, and it took the bishop himself to organise an army and see them off [5]. The British monk Gildas, writing sometime around the 540s, paints a more extreme picture of ethnic cleansing bordering on genocide. He depicts this as culminating in an appeal for help to "Agitus, thrice consul", the governor still defending the imperial cause in Gaul:

The barbarians drive us to the sea, the sea drives us upon the barbarians; by one or the other of these two kinds of death we are either killed or drowned. [6].

The English monk Bede, writing two centuries later in 731 , corrects the name to Aetius and dates the appeal to the year 446, which is known to be within the consul's third period of office. He also implies that the appeal was unsuccessful because he then tells us that:

In the year of our Lord 449.... the race of the Angles or Saxons , invited by Vortigern [the British 'overlord'] came to Britain in three warships and by his command were granted a place of settlement in the eastern part of the island, ostensibly to fight on behalf of the country, but their real intention was to conquer it....at once a much larger force was sent over with a stronger band of warriors; this, added to the contingent already there, made an invincible army.....They came from three very powerful Germanic tribes, the Saxons, Angles and Jutes. The people of Kent and the inhabitants of the Isle of Wight are of Jutish origin....From the Saxon country , that is, the district now known as Old Saxony, came the East Saxons, the South Saxons [my emphasis] *and the West Saxons. Besides this, from the country of the Angles....came the East Angles, the Middle Angles, the Mercians, and all the Northumbrian race (that is those people who dwell north of the river Humber).* [7]

Bede tells us elsewhere[8] that subsequently Wessex absorbed the Isle of Wight, and he implies that in the midlands Mercia did likewise with Middle Anglia, creating the well known 'heptarchy' or seven kingdoms of Northumbria, Mercia, East Anglia, Wessex, Kent, Essex and Sussex.

So from this it might be concluded that Sussex is one of only three English counties that can trace their way back to the status of kingdom, particularly as the 'shiring' or division of the larger kingdoms into the counties familiar to us did not occur until much later, eg about the year 700 in Wessex and two centuries later than that in Mercia[9]. However, Bede and other sources, together with the evidence of place names, suggest that a number of other counties were or may have been kingdoms very early on, *before* getting absorbed into one of the large kingdoms. This applies with varying degrees of certainty to Yorkshire (*Deira*), Lincolnshire (*Lindiswara*), Middlesex (*Middel Seaxa*), Surrey (*Su ri*, or south of the river) and Gloucestershire (*Hwicce*), besides Cornwall and Cumbria, which have their origins in post-Roman Celtic British kingdoms absorbed several centuries later into England (so leaving Wales as the only redoubt of the Britons). Safe to say, however, that Sussex is one of no more than at most ten counties that have their origins well before the process that created all the ' - shires', almost certainly in the earliest stage of Anglo-Saxon settlement.

As we have seen, Bede suggests a foundation sometime not long after the year 450. He also tells us [10] that while King Aethelbert of Kent (reigned 560–616) was the third overlord of all the southern kingdoms, and the second had been King Ceawlin of the West Saxons (circa mid sixth century) the first had been King Aella of the South Saxons (presumably first half of the sixth century). This may seem odd given the size of Sussex, but it should be remembered that the larger kingdoms were still embryonic at this stage, and that the position may have been more that of a war co-ordinator appointed by agreement than of a dominant high king.

Another account of the establishment of Sussex, which while providing a little more detail is much later, is the *Anglo-Saxon Chronicle* instituted by King Alfred in the late ninth century . We do not know how early, or how reliable, its sources (other than Bede) may be. After broadly following Bede's account of the establishment of the first Anglo-Saxon kingdom, Kent, which it places in the year 455, it continues:

477 *Aella came to Britain, and his three sons Cymen, Wlencing and Cyssa, with three ships, landing at the place called Cymensora. There they killed many Welsh and drove some in flight into The Weald.*

485 *Aella fought the Welsh on the bank near Mercredesburna.*

491 *Aella and Cyssa besieged Anderida, near Pevensey, and killed all who were inside, so there was not one Briton left.* [11].

The similarly violent arrival of Cerdic and Cynric to found Wessex is then recorded for 495, though there is no narrative for the founding of any other kingdom.

A number of points should be understood about this. We cannot be sure about the dating, in a document written so long after the events, but it is not inconsistent with Gildas and Bede to place the *adventus saxonum* or arrival of the Anglo-Saxons in the mid–late fifth century (though some scholars favour an early fifth century and/or a more gradual process). Secondly, the names Wlencing and Cyssa may have been invented to link with the place names Lancing and Cissbury, as is clearly the case where the *Chronicle* introduces Port as the founder of Portsmouth, a word which actually derives from the Roman name for that city. Mercredesburna means 'river of the agreed frontier', which suggests a drive eastwards along the Sussex coast, a cessation of fighting with a river (the Arun , Adur or Ouse?) as a boundary, and then a further push towards the massacre in the Roman fort at Pevensey. The earlier flight of Britons into the Weald suggests that Aella's territory was initially only the coastal strip and the Downland slopes and valleys behind it, not the dense woodland (nowadays farmland) that lay to the north.

It seems that the historical details will always remain uncertain, but there is also an older and even more intriguing mystery: what evidence is there that Sussex pre-existed as a Roman province? Many modern sources, for example Todd [12] and Morris [13], simply indicate that the area broadly corresponding to Sussex in Roman times was occupied by the *Regini* or *Regnenses* and was administered from *Noviomagus Regnensium* (Chichester) by, in the first century, a client King called Cogidubnus. But from Miles Russell's specialised analysis of Sussex in the Roman period [14] it appears that this is leaping to a lot of conclusions. All we actually know is that:

- Tribal capitals all had a town name followed by the genitive case (ie 'of the') of the tribe inhabiting the territory. For example those surrounding Sussex were *Venta Belgarum* (Winchester) in south Hampshire, administering the *Belgae*; *Calleva Atrebatum* (Silchester) in north Hampshire, administering the Atrebates; and *Durovernum Cantiacorum* (Canterbury) in Kent, administering the *Cantiaci*.

- *Noviomagus Regnensium* would, on the same principle, indicate the administrative centre of a tribe called the *Regini*, *Regni* or *Regnenses*. I can find no direct references to these people, and while there could have been such a tribe, any of the terms could translate from Latin as '(the people) of the *Regnum*', or kingdom.

- There is a first century inscription, excavated and displayed in Chichester, honouring the emperor's family, in the name of Cogidubnus, *"rex magnus"* (great king).

- The late first century Roman historian Tacitus tells us that soon after the Roman conquest:

  Certain domains were presented to King Cogidumnus, who maintained his unswerving loyalty right down to our own times - an example of the long-established Roman custom of employing even kings to make others slaves. [15]

  Tacitus does not tell us where these domains were, except that the overall imperial province was being established in "the nearest parts of Britain", ie presumably the south-east.

- In 1960 the remains of Fishbourne Roman palace, two miles west of Chichester, were first discovered. The building, which originated in the first century, is much more extensive and lavish than any other known Roman dwelling in Britain, being definitely a palace rather than a villa, and suggesting occupation by a king (albeit one that was a client of the Romans).

It therefore seems likely that the Regini or Regnenses were not a tribe but a section of one, or a breakaway group, which had welcomed rather than resisted the Roman invasion, and whose leader (Cogidubnus or Cogidumnus) was therefore made a client-king and allowed to administer a territory from Chichester known as 'the Kingdom'. There are other examples, of course, ranging from Boadicea's husband King Prasutagus in East Anglia to King Herod at the other end of the Empire.

If this is accepted, the question then arises as to how far this territory coincided with the subsequent area of Sussex. The proximity of Winchester and Silchester to Chichester suggests that Chichester's territory could not have extended significantly into modern-day Hampshire, and by the same token it seems unlikely that their authority would have stretched very far into land closer to Chichester than themselves, ie any part of West Sussex.

This would suggest a western border of Regnum very close to the current Sussex-Hampshire boundary. The kingdom would certainly therefore have covered part at least of West Sussex, perhaps focused on the corridor from Chichester towards London, centred on Stane Street, which is rich in the remains of Roman villas, military stations and other outposts. The situation regarding East Sussex (whose known Roman settlements are confined to its south-western corner and south coast, though in the north and east close to Kent there are remains of much iron working) is unclear. It is also not known whether any part of Surrey might have fallen within Chichester's orbit, though much of that county is geographically closer to Silchester.

An entity called Regnum, based at Chichester, comprising some or all of West Sussex, and not extending into Hampshire or Kent, is therefore likely. But how far it extended into East Sussex, and/or into Surrey, and so how far it was a true precursor of Sussex, remains a mystery.

2 HOW DID CHRISTIANITY COME TO SUSSEX?

On the face it, there appears to be no mystery at least about the initial arrival of Christianity in Sussex. Bede provides a detailed account of St Augustine's mission from Rome to Kent in the year 597, and missions from there to Essex, Northumbria, East Anglia and Wessex with (except in Wessex) various setbacks due to 'regime change'. Equally he narrates the mission in 635 from the Celtic church of Iona, in the Hebrides (itself established a little earlier by the Irish saint Columba), to Northumbria, and its spreading of the new faith to Mercia and elsewhere where the Roman mission had not entirely prevailed. He recounts how the conversion of most of England highlighted differences of practice between Celtic and Roman Christianity, which, while not concerning doctrine, appear to have been significant as a marker of papal authority.[16]

It would seem that either the church in Britain and Ireland, while in some isolation because of the pagan Anglo-Saxons, had lost its sense of taking direction from the bishop of Rome; or that at the time of its foundation two-three centuries earlier, the authority of the pope had been more a matter of esteem than of direct power, and the Celts had not 'moved with the times'.

Bede then relates the proceedings of the Synod of Whitby in 663, called to determine whether the English church would follow the Celtic or the Roman custom, and the decision in favour of the latter. The principle advocate for the winning side was Wilfrid, the abbot of Hexham (near Hadrian's Wall) who was made bishop of York (ie with authority over all Northumbria) the following year. We are told that he travelled to Gaul for consecration, presumably to avoid the possibility of any bishops with a Celtic provenance being involved.

Bede then tells us that Wilfrid, who appears to have been an energetic but argumentative man, fell out with the next king of Northumbria in 678 and went into exile. Bede continues:

Though he could not be received back into his own native land and his diocese, owing to the hostility of King Ecgfrith, yet nothing could hinder him from the ministry of preaching the gospel. So he turned to the kingdom of the South Saxons, which stretches south and west from Kent as far as the land of the West Saxons and contains 7000 hides. At that time it was still in the bonds of heathen practices. Here Wilfrid taught them the faith and administered the baptism of salvation. [17]

So for some reason Sussex, despite adjoining Kent where Augustine's mission had started in 597, had been overlooked or ignored in the process of the conversion of England and remained pagan 80 years on – until a dismissed and restless bishop from Yorkshire was seeking a new challenge. Bede makes it clear, though, that Wilfrid was not arriving like Dr Livingstone in completely fresh pastures. Firstly, the king of Sussex, Aethelwealh, had a Christian queen from the Hwicce people (in the Gloucestershire area); and he had himself recently been baptised in Mercia under the influence of its king, Wulfhere.

Wilfrid's work was undertaken 'with the king's consent and indeed to his great joy'. [17] Secondly, there was already "in their midst a certain Irish monk named Dicuill, who had a very small monastery in a place called Bosham surrounded by woods and sea, in which five or six brothers served the Lord in humility and poverty; but none of the natives cared to follow their way of life or listen to their preaching." [18]. Bosham lies on an inlet of Chichester harbour and the church and village are still to this day surrounded by woods and sea.

It is, howeverk a shock to any son or daughter of Sussex to grasp that while Christianity and its associated literacy and learning was flourishing in places like York and Hexham, not to mention Glasgow and the Hebrides, it had not really penetrated Sussex, albeit that the coast of Christian Europe was only 70 miles distant. Secondly, the success of Irish missionaries in the north and midlands of England could suggest a possibly parochial xenophobia in the South Saxons' refusal to respond to Dicuill, preferring instead to await the arrival of an English missionary. But the most sobering thought is provoked by Bede's account of the famine in Sussex at the time of Wilfrid's arrival. The saint taught them how to fish, of which they had had "no knowledge", (!) and the consequent alleviation of widespread hunger "won the hearts of all", [19] so disposing them to respond favourably to Wilfrid's message.

So, it might be asked, where is the mystery? Part of the answer is whether or not a much earlier visit by Wilfred to Sussex took place; and if it did, why does Bede, who had access to people who had known Wilfrid [20] make no reference to it? Besides Bede we have a detailed biography of Wilfrid written by a monk called Eddius Stephanus in the year 720, ie eleven years after the saint died and eleven years before Bede's *Ecclesiastical History*. Stephanus's short account of the conversion of Sussex is similar to Bede's except that he has the saint converting King Aethelwealh and his queen before proceeding to evangelise the population, instead of the royal couple being Christians already as in Bede. He also adds that the king gave Wilfrid land at Selsey (on the coast near Chichester) for his episcopal seat, where the saint founded a "community" of "brethren" [21] before departing to pursue his reinstatement in Northumbria.

However, earlier in the book [22] Stephanus relates an event fifteen years before, in 666, when Wilfrid and his companions were returning from his consecration in Gaul. He relates that the ship was overtaken by a violent storm which drove it towards the coast of "the land of the South Saxons, a region quite unknown to them". The ship was thrown up on to the shore, when suddenly the water retreated, leaving it beached. The party was attacked by a great horde of people intent on looting the ship and enslaving or killing its occupants, but the group fought back killing the pagans' chief priest with a stone from a sling shot, like David and Goliath. They inflicted losses on their attackers but, just as the crowd was regrouping to overwhelm them, the sea flowed back and they were able to cast off and sail away.

It is a puzzle why Bede does not relate this. It is possible that he did not know of Stephanus's book, although, as mentioned above, he had contact with other people who had known Wilfrid and who surely would have known about such a key incident. It might be that the story was not confirmed by anyone else and he thought it was unreliable, for it does have elements of hagiography; Bede for example is more likely to be reliable on not breathlessly crediting Wilfrid with the conversion of the king. Or it is possible that Bede may have omitted the story, feeling that an initial contact in which Wilfrid's party kills some of the South Saxons (albeit in self defence) rather than converts them did not reflect well on the saint.

It seems we will never know the truth. Both narratives (Stephanus's stone-throwing battle and later royal grant of land at Selsey, and Bede's lesson to the South Saxons on fishing) are interestingly combined in an early twentieth century poem in dialect by W. Victor Cook entitled *Sussex Won't be Druv*. This appeared as the prologue in E.V. Lucas's classic book on Sussex [23]. The poem's three verses are about the dogged yet lovable obstinacy of Sussex people, and the middle verse relates:

> Mus' Wilfrid came to Selsey.
> Us heaved a stone at he,
> Because he rackoned he could teach
> Our Sussex fishers how to reach
> The fishes in the sea.
> But when he dwelt among us,
> Us gave un land and love,
> For Sussex will be Sussex,
> And Sussex won't be druv.

As for the subsequent spreading of Christianity in Sussex after Wilfrid's departure, we have intriguingly very little information. There is a well-established story of St Cuthman, which appears in many sources (for example, E.V. Lucas's book mentioned above [24]) some of which attribute it to a book of lives of the saints called *Acta Sanctorum*, published in 1658. The tale relates that the saint was born at about the time of Wilfrid's mission, either in Wessex or at Chidham, near Chichester. As a young shepherd he was called away from care of his sheep and so drew a circle around them on the ground with his crook, within which they remained during his absence. On his father's death he left home and headed eastwards, pulling his elderly and infirm mother behind him in a wheelbarrow. At one point the rope over his shoulders with which he was pulling the wheelbarrow broke in front of a group of haymakers, who unkindly laughed: their crop was at once ruined by a sudden storm. When the rope broke a second time Cuthman took this as a divine sign that he should build the church that he had planned there, which he did – the place being the village of Steyning on the river Adur, in the eastern part of West Sussex. The church was replaced by the current splendid Norman building in the twelfth century, the dedication to St Andrew possibly replacing an earlier one to Cuthman. Happily, however, the church added Cuthman to the dedication in 2009, following the earlier dedication of a chapel to him and a window honouring him. A striking modern statue of him by sculptor Penelope Reeve now also stands just across the road from the churchyard.

Otherwise the spread of Christianity in Sussex remains obscure. I argue below (Chapter 7) that Dicuill, when supplanted by Wilfrid as the principal (and royally authorised) champion of Christianity with a base in the west of the territory, might have decamped to Ditchling thirty five miles to the east, but this is speculation based solely on place name resemblance.

An oral tradition of a St Brighthelm as the bringer of the faith to Brighton (on old maps Brighthelmstone) was commonly related in local schools in my childhood, but has proved very difficult to find in any written source. The only such confirmation I have tracked down is in a nineteenth century history of the town, which says:

The name doubtless was derived from St Brighthelm, a Saxon Bishop, who gave the name to the town, and who resided here during the Heptarchy, for we find that Ella with his three sons (Cimen, Wlencing and Cissa) effected their landing at West Wittering, south west of Chichester, A.D. 447. . . Brighthelm accompanied this army [25].

This seems to be based on the account of the foundation of Sussex in the *Anglo-Saxon Chronicle* quoted in Chapter 1 above, though the date given in that source is 477, and there is no reference in it to the site of the landing, given as *Cymensora* (Cymen's shore), being necessarily West Wittering. The claim that Bishop Brighthelm accompanied Aella's army is clearly an anachronism, as this pre-dates Wilfrid's Christian mission to pagan Sussex by two centuries! If it were true, it would make Brighton the cradle of English Christianity (instead of Canterbury from 597), which it clearly was not. So we have virtually no knowledge of how Christianity spread to eastern Sussex.

Even more strikingly, while there is evidence of Christianity in Roman Britain (albeit extinguished by the pagan Anglo-Saxons) in the remains of household chapels at Lullingstone in Kent and Hinton St Mary in Dorset, and possibly a church at Silchester, there is no such evidence in Sussex. The time when Christianity was preached or practised for the very first time in the area therefore remains unknown.

3 THE LONG MAN OF WILMINGTON

Of all the mysteries in Sussex, the Long Man of Wilmington is perhaps the best known and most mysterious. Wilmington is a village below (ie immediately north of) the eastern South Downs, about six miles inland from Eastbourne. The known facts about the Long Man are few and are well summarised on the Sussex Past website [26] of the Sussex Archeological Trust, to whom the site was gifted in 1925. The figure is a white outline of a man, without features or protrusions, on the grass of the steep north-facing escarpment of Windover Hill in the South Downs. He is 235ft high, his arms are half outstretched, and in each hand he has a vertical pole about the same height as himself.

It is claimed that he is the largest representation of the human figure in Europe, but there appears to be no official confirmation of this. This is perhaps the mystery about him which could be most easily solved. There is no known reference to the Long Man until a drawing of 1710, by a surveyor, John Rowley. This shows the figure with facial features and possibly wearing a helmet, which could suggest a war god. Originally the figure was only a slight indentation in the grass, visible only in certain conditions, for example when the sun was at a certain angle, which might explain the lack of earlier references. In 1874, however, the figure was restored and marked by yellow bricks, which were temporarily painted green during the Second World War for camouflage, and which were then replaced by the current white-ish cement blocks in 1969.

The compelling mystery about the Long Man is when he was carved, and by whom, and for what purpose. The different possibilities are carefully considered in Chapter 8 of *Lost Gods of Albion* [27], to which the next part of this chapter is indebted.

Firstly, the drawings. The next illustration (overleaf) was drawn by Sir William Burrell in 1776 and shows the figure still with facial features (and indications of these were confirmed in an excavation by Sir Flinders Petrie in 1926).

Drawing by John Rowley, 1710.
[Reproduced by permission of Chatsworth Settlement Trustees]

However in the second drawing:

• He is now without any suggestion of a helmet, but with hair indicated on his head;

• His feet point down to the left and right respectively, compared with the earlier Rowley drawing where they point straight out either side (and today when they both point down and slightly to the figure's right)

• The two staves either side have acquired tool heads to become a rake and a scythe respectively (whereas earlier, in 1710, and now they are simply vertical lines).

• The figure does not have any visible neck (again unlike the earlier 1710 drawing, and now).

• Below the chin there is a V-neck opening, which gives the impression that the figure is clad in a sort of all-in-one romper suit (again unlike the earlier 1710 drawing, and now).

The first two differences, the top of the head and the direction of the feet, could be explained by changes made to the figure between 1710 and 1776, and then more changes between 1776 and when it assumed its current form in 1874. Or they could just be two observers in 1710 and 1776 straining to make out details from the same faint indentations in the grass, and coming to different interpretations. **But the third, fourth and fifth points above are mysterious, because in each case the 1710 drawing and the current appearance agree, and the 1776 drawing fundamentally differs**.

This can only be explained either by Sir William Burrell for some reason inventing these details; or by someone adding the hair, rake-head, scythe-head and V-neck between 1710 and 1776, and then someone removing them some time between 1776 and 1874.

This would seem to be a remarkable coincidence unless the latter person – making changes in the late eighteenth

Drawing Sir William Burrell, 1776.

century or the nineteenth century – knew of the appearance in the early eighteenth century and was amending the figure to go back to it. *But since the 1710 drawing was only discovered (at Chatsworth House in Yorkshire) in 1993, up until when the earliest known drawing was the 1776 one,* it is difficult to see how a later restorer could have known which features were eighteenth century additions and so to be reversed.

Other notable facts about the Long Man is that he is elongated, which compensates for the approximately 28 degree slope of the hillside, so that from ground level he appears to be in normal proportion. Secondly, a rectangle around him appears to be flattened compared with the natural rounded nature of the hillside. Thirdly, during the 1874 restoration, fragments of Roman brick were reportedly found when the topsoil was removed in order to slot in the yellow bricks, according to the local press,[28] though unfortunately no specimens are known to exist and no other confirmation is known. Fourthly, the 1969 restoration confirmed the belief that the original outline was created by cutting away the top soil to reveal the chalk below, which if untended would naturally silt up and grass over again in time, leaving only a slight indentation in the grass. That restoration too found possible traces of what could have been a scythe blade and the teeth of a rake at the respective tops of the staves, which would give some support to the Burrell drawing of 1776. Finally, the 1969 exercise produced some ground-up pieces of fired clay used as filler in the small part of the incised outline that was excavated : academics from the University of Southampton who examined them thought they were more likely to be Roman than prehistoric, though they could not be certain.

So what is the age of the Long Man? A prehistoric origin, like other chalk hill figures in southern England such as the Uffington White Horse, is clearly a strong possibility. It is supported by the presence on the hilltop nearby of Neolithic and Bronze Age barrows, and the possibility remains that the ground-up fired clay discovered in 1969 was prehistoric, albeit that a Roman origin for them was thought more likely.

An origin in Roman times would be suggested if either the ground brick fragments reportedly found in 1874, or the ground pottery fragments found in 1969, had been confirmed as Roman. But as we have seen, a Roman date has not been proved for either. Also of course Roman material might have been used in a restoration or adaptation of the figure during the Roman period, its origin in that case still lying in pre-history. A Roman provenance of either kind is suggested by the similarity of the Long Man to the reverse of a coin of the emperor Vetranio (reigned AD 350), showing a figure with half-outstretched arms bearing vertical staves, at the top of which are two almost square banners.

It seems a possibility that if the inscribed objects at the top of the Long Man's staves existed, they could have been the remains of such banners rather than the rake-head and scythe-head that they have been interpreted to be. Even if the banners on the coin are Christian in nature, as suggested by Paul Newman [29], the origin and purpose of the figure could well have been military rather than religious, and as such representative of an older pagan tradition.

I can find no link made by any author between the Long Man and the phenomenon nearby that definitely is of late Roman origin, the ancient yew tree in the churchyard at Wilmington. A certificate in the church porch says that this has been authoritatively dated to around the year AD 400, which must surely make it one of the oldest in England. It is a splendid sight, with its long enormous arms too heavy for the gnarled and aged trunk, and so supported by wooden posts. Many country churchyards in England have an ancient yew, and explanations vary from the toxin of the leaves deterring farmers from allowing their animals to stray in, to a theory that as evergreens they symbolise eternal life and therefore mark early places of worship – either Christian sites or pagan ones later taken over by Christianity. By the year 400 the Roman empire had been officially Christian for three quarters of a century, but the interlude of Julian the Apostate (emperor AD 360–363) shows that paganism was by no means eradicated. The yew tree could therefore have been planted by Christians, or by (dissident) pagan Romans, or by pagan Britons just after the end of the officially Christian regime around 409. Similar possibilities apply to the Long Man, though no link between them can be proven. The churchyard lies roughly north-north-east of the Long Man, so there is no directional link as would have been suggested by, say, an exact north-south alignment.

As well as similarity with the Roman coin, the Long Man also bears a striking resemblance to a figure on a bronze belt buckle excavated in 1964 from a pagan Anglo-Saxon cemetery at Finglesham in Kent. [30] The figure has half-

Coin of the Roman emperor Vetriana, AD 350 [Wikipedia – Creative Commons]

outstretched arms and a spear in each hand, and although these bow at the top slightly out from the vertical, this appears to be in order to follow the inverted triangle shape of the buckle. Of course the buckle image itself might have been derived from the Roman prototype on the coin, perhaps taken as loot or received in payment for military service prior to the Anglo-Saxon revolt described by Gildas and Bede. A Roman origin for the powdered filler excavated from the Long Man in 1969 would also not rule out an Anglo-Saxon provenance for the figure, since Roman pottery fragments and bricks remained around long after the collapse of empire (for example Roman tiles re-used in St. Albans Abbey).

There is a possibility of a medieval origin, and some commentators have speculated that the monks of Wilmington Priory (dissolved in 1414) may have been responsible. The figure hardly seems, however, to conform to a spirit of Christian devotion that one would expect from this period in general and from a monastic origin in particular.

Finally, in 2002-04 a team of researchers from the University of Reading applied thermo-luminescence dating to brick fragments that once enclosed the Long Man. The approximate date indicated by the tests was AD 1545, suggesting perhaps a Tudor folly. [31] It seems to me, though, that this can hardly be conclusive. The figure could equally have had a much older origin, and have been marked out in Tudor times, just as it was in 1874 and 1969. Thermo-luminescence dating of fragments of the yellow bricks placed in 1874, or of the cement blocks placed in 1969, would most certainly not prove that the figure originated on those dates. On the other hand, the fact that the figure is elongated to compensate for the slope of the hillside, so that he appears of normal proportions from the village, at ground level, suggests a knowledge of perspective that developed only in the renaissance. Unless some Neolithic or bronze age hill figure artists had greater knowledge than we might think . . .

The purpose of the figure, if we could divine it, could shed light on the period of origin. If, as has been suggested by some, he is a god opening the gates of dawn (ie the vertical lines in his hands are not staves but doors), then the purpose might be one of evoking fertility for a successful harvest. The same would be true if the staves, as interpreted by Sir William Burrell in 1776 and Sir Flinders Petrie in 1926, were a rake and a scythe. If however they are banners, as on the Roman coin, or

The Finglesham belt buckle. [Wikipedia – Creative Commons]

spears, as on the Anglo-Saxon belt buckle, the likelihood is that he is a war god – created either to celebrate or invoke victory in a general sense, or to overawe a subject or nearby hostile population. Finally, of course, a pastiche in Tudor times could have been meant to copy any of these.

What seems least likely is that he is a medieval creation, since his appearance in no way appears to relate to Christian iconography but clearly has a pagan reference. An early origin begs the question of why the figure was not documented until 1710, but society before the 'age of reason' may have had little interest in indentations in the ground made by primitive precursors. Or there may be earlier references (bearing in mind that the 1776 drawing was thought to be the oldest until the 1710 one was discovered) which are lost or unknown to us.

My personal inclination is towards a pagan Anglo-Saxon origin. The Long Man has a remarkable similarity to the figure on the Finglesham belt buckle, and his primeval force seems more akin to a barbarian than a classical version of paganism. Moreover his position, on the north escarpment of the South Downs, could mark the northern limit of Aelle's territory as he reportedly advanced eastwards towards Pevensey in the late fifth century, driving the Britons "in flight into the Weald". [11] A war god to overawe those Britons and discourage them from counter-attacking south from the Weald and over the Downs would give a practical, as well as a ritual, purpose for such a figure.

That he had a ritual function is, in my view, made likely by the existence of a mound at the bottom of the figure. It is an irregular oval with a reasonably flat top, measuring about 30 yards from east to west and about 20 yards from north to south. On its south side, facing the figure, it lies alongside the east-west path running below the Long Man, but otherwise its sides descend steeply to the surrounding hillside. My compass reading indicated that the head and 'heart' of the Long Man lie due south from where a steep path up the side of the mound reaches its surface – in other words the entrance to the mound lies due north of the Long Man.

On a day in early February sometime around 2005 or 2006 I approached the figure on the upward path that leads to it from the village, and saw a group of people chatting informally on the mound. On reaching the mound top myself, I noticed that some were wearing dark cloaks, and that a home-baked loaf of bread and a flagon of cider had been laid near the periphery closest to the Long Man. I believe these might have been the Anderida Gorsedd, a group of modern druids whose website [32] indicates that they have celebrated the turning of the seasons at the site since 2003. It seems likely that they had pagan predecessors who created the Long Man and honoured him from this spot, though whether they were Neolithic, Bronze age, Roman or Anglo-Saxon – or merely Tudors creating an artifice – remains to puzzle us.

4 LULLINGTON CHURCH

Lullington Church lies about a mile east of the Long Man, and can be reached from it by the footpath that runs below the figure, westwards along the side of the Downs, and then by joining the lane from Wilmington towards Litlington on the river Cuckmere. The church stands back from this lane, on the hillside, but is hidden by two cottages and their gardens , and a narrow but dense ring of woodland which loops around. The visitor, leaving the lane by the taking the 'twitten' or path between the high garden walls and the trees, therefore comes upon the churchyard suddenly, having had no view while approaching. Similarly, once having left, there is no backward or distant view to confirm or give context to one's visit. A gap in the trees gives a view from the church over fields descending westwards towards the river, with Berwick Church's steeple in the distance, and Firle beacon further still; but the churchyard nevertheless feels like a 'bubble' outside the normal flow of life and time.

The few known facts about the church are helpfully set out in the guide booklet for St Andrew's Church, Alfriston (the 'Cathedral of the Downs') in a section towards the end about its much smaller but no less beautiful neighbour. [33]

The church is about sixteen feet square, topped by a shingle roof and a tiny weather-boarded belfry and octagonal spire. It is clearly only the chancel of the original church, the foundations of some of the nave walls being visible to its west. There is a tradition the nave was burnt down in Cromwellian times. The building dates from the thirteenth century, in the simple and homely Early English style which beautifully suits a modest size and which is typical of many Downland churches. It was transferred from the ownership of Battle Abbey to Richard de la Wych (Saint Richard), Bishop of Chichester, in 1251. The guide booklet continues:

The original dedication is not known and there may never have been one, but Jegelian Hunt in his will dated 1521, among the other bequests to the church: "I will a taper sett before Saint Sithe in the same church". Who Saint Sithe was is uncertain. In 1998 plans were set up to provide Lullington Church with a dedication. After extensive consultation it was decided that "The Church of the Good Shepherd" was most appropriate for this tiny church high on the Downs. The Bishop of Lewes conducted the dedication on 10th September 2000. [34]

An older version of the guide adds, after the reference to Saint Sithe, that she might have been "the Saint Sitha, the maidservant of Lucca, held in veneration by English housewives, rather than the Saxon martyred princess Saint Osyth". Finally the guide ends with yet another tantalising piece of information:

An interesting note appeared in the Sussex County Magazine, Vol. 9, 1935, regarding Lullington Church. It reads: "We understand from a Sussex architect that a replica of Lullington Church was erected in the U.S.A. as a war memorial, but he is unable to give details without permission of his clients." It would be very interesting to know where this was erected and by whom. [35]

The mysteries surrounding Lullington Church are therefore as abundant as its size is small:

• Is it, at sixteen feet square, the smallest church in England?

• To which saint was it originally dedicated, ie St Sitha, St Osyth or someone else, and when and how was the dedication lost?

• How did the church originate, given that it seems to serve no village (and a former village is unlikely, as a hillside settlement would be unusual in the Downs)? The road past it is called Chapel Hill, suggesting a chapel-of-ease rather than a parish church, but if this was for local shepherds it is notable that

Wilmington, Alfriston and Litlington churches are all within only one mile. Was it perhaps a chapel for the convenience of the owners of Lullington Court or Lullington Manor nearby?

• When, why and by whom was the chancel destroyed - was it during the English Civil War, as believed, and if it was by parliamentary forces why would they vandalise it rather than adapt it for puritan worship as elsewhere?

• Could there be any link between this destruction and the loss or erasure of the dedication?

• Was a replica erected in the 1930s in the USA, and if so where, and by whom, and why has there never been any information about it?

And there are still further mysteries surrounding this beautiful and numinous place. About a year after my encounter with the druids or pagans at the Long Man I visited again, following a walk I often do in early February because of the first appearance of snowdrops at that time of year in wooded parts of the whole area from Folkington to Berwick. I was careful, however, to time my visit for 2nd February, reasoning that as this is Candlemas, overlying an earlier Celtic festival (six and a half weeks after the winter solstice, and six and a half weeks before the spring equinox, the full thirteen weeks being a quarter of the year) it was the most likely date for me to see the worshippers again. Sadly I saw no sign of them. But on continuing to Lullington I found a strange sight. Of the few gravestones dotted about the churchyard, two are just inside the wooded grove which forms its boundary (it having no wall). On the bare branches of a tree overhanging one of the gravestones was a profusion of seashells, each hanging by a coloured strand of cotton looping through a small hole made in the middle of the shell. They were shaking and dancing in the icy wind, above a carpet of snowdrops under the trees. I have visited several times since, mostly at this time of year, but have never seen this since.

However, the other phenomenon at the same spot remains. It is the low stump of a tree, about three feet high and in the shape of a figure 7, clearly sawn off at the end. The horizontal part is for some reason caked in earth from which springs a thick profusion of small branches, stems and greenery, like the head of a hydra. The whole appearance is rather sinister; but as such it is in contrast to the church itself, whose little interior has a compelling atmosphere. The visitors' book is full of comments from people struggling to express a feeling of being deeply moved, and although the place is beautiful it is not easy to explain why it should so often have this profound effect.

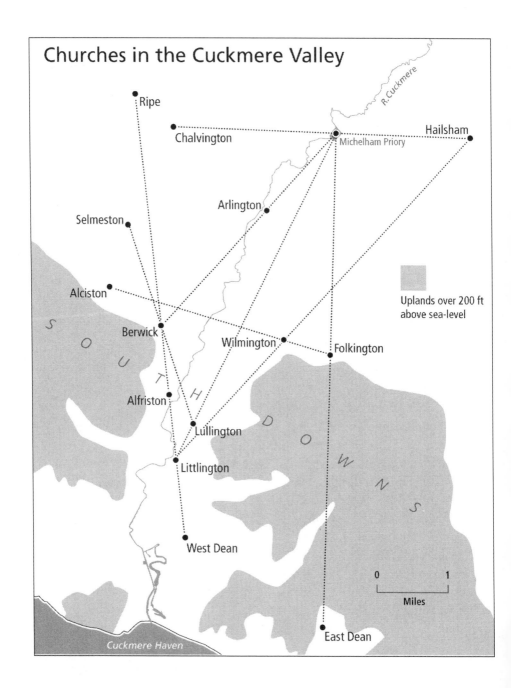

Churches in the Cuckmere Valley

Ripe

Chalvington

Hailsham

Michelham Priory

R.Cuckmere

Arlington

Selmeston

Alciston

Uplands over 200 ft
above sea-level

Berwick

Wilmington

Folkington

S O U T H

Alfriston

Lullington

Littlington

D O W N S

West Dean

0   1

Miles

East Dean

Cuckmere Haven

5 LEY LINES IN SUSSEX?

Lullington Church is also part of a wider mystery – is there evidence of ley lines in Sussex? Ley lines, as is widely known, are supposed straight lines across the landscape linking sacred places. The points linked are most often churches, the belief being that Christian churches were frequently built on the site of earlier pagan places of worship (as famously by the Anglo-Saxon missionary St Boniface in Germany). [36]

The river Cuckmere really grows from a stream to a river near the village of Hellingly, and after many meanders it enters the sea about twelve miles south-west of this point at Cuckmere Haven. Four ancient churches – Michelham Priory, Arlington, Alfriston and Litlington – lie within yards of the river. A further eleven lie within two miles either side of the river, namely Hailsham, Chalvington, Ripe, Selmeston, Alciston, Berwick, Wilmington, Lullington, West Dean, Folkington amd East Dean. These fifteen places are therefore distributed randomly (in a mathematical sense) in the rectangle twelve miles by four, formed as suggested above, which constitutes the valley of the river as it flows south-westwards through the South Downs. Ordnance Survey Landranger map, 1¼ inches to 1 mile, no.199 shows the area.

The fifteen points yield seven straight lines that each link three churches, viz:

Chalvington – Michelham Priory – Hailsham
Michelham Priory – Arlington – Berwick
Michelham Priory – Lullington – Litlington
Michelham Priory – Folkington – East Dean
Hailsham – Wilmington – Litlington
Alciston – Wilmington – Folkington
Selmeston – Berwick – Lullington

In addition one straight line links five churches, viz:

Ripe – Berwick – Alfriston – Litlington – West Dean

Altogether therefore Michelham Priory features on four of the lines, Berwick and Litlington on three, Hailsham and Lullington on two, and the remainder on one. The northernmost church in the area, Hellingly, does not, however, feature on a line. Neither does the Long Man of Wilmington, though various websites devoted to ley lines link it with prehistoric barrows and other features.

It may be that a mathematician could calculate the probability of these alignments occurring by chance, but to a lay person they do seem unlikely to have occurred other than by design. In this context it could be helpful to compare other clusters of churches in defined areas. The most obvious to examine would be the valley of the next river which flows through the Downs, the Ouse. This rises south of Horsham, and on its journey for twenty miles or more eastwards through the High Weald only half a dozen ancient churches lie near it, and they are not linked by any straight lines.

The same is true of the five churches on the middle stretch of the river, in the Low Weald. As the river nears the town of Lewes, however (where it starts to go through the South Downs) three neighbouring village churches, Barcombe, Hamsey and Malling, can be joined by a straight line. This seemed to me to suggest that the handful of medieval churches in Lewes, and the ten which lie close to the eight mile final stretch of the Ouse between Lewes and the sea, might yield an abundant crop of straight lines. The fact is, however, that this rectangle of eight miles by four, which might be drawn to approximate to the lower Ouse valley, has no straight lines at all to join its relatively dense cluster of churches.

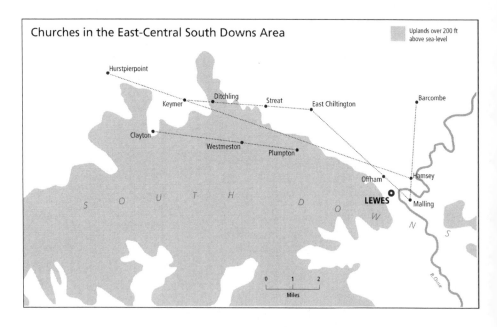

Churches in the East-Central South Downs Area

Uplands over 200 ft above sea-level

N/A

What can we conclude from this? Firstly, it does show that a cluster of a dozen or more points within a few square miles, such as those in the lower Cuckmere and lower Ouse valleys, does not mathematically have to yield a bunch of straight lines joining them in threes (or more). The possibility of human design where straight lines do occur therefore remains open. But it also leaves open the possibility that, where there is such a cluster, sometimes quite a lot of straight lines can occur by chance and sometimes only a few or none.

However, the position near Lewes is a bit more complicated. The Barcombe – Hamsey – Malling line runs roughly north to south down the river, immediately above Lewes. At this point the river forms the eastern boundary of an area that can be discerned as the plain immediately north of the line of the South Downs. A natural rectangular area can be identified running about nine miles westwards along the bottom of the Downs from Lewes to the next gap in the hills, the A23 (London – Brighton) road, and extending 2–3 miles to the north. This area is essentially the springline of the Downs, where rainwater that has soaked through the chalk of the hills hits harder rock below and emerges at the foot of the hills as springs. As such it is prolific in villages along the bottom of the hills, sited to take advantage of the water supply, and also the opportunity for pasture on the hillside above and crops on the flat land immediately to the north.

This perceived rectangle, about nine miles by three (which may be seen on Ordnance Survey Landranger map, 1¼ inches to 1 mile, no. 198) contains straight line links in addition to Barcombe – Hamsey – Malling of:

Hamsey – Keymer – Hurstpierpoint
Malling – Offham – East Chiltington
Plumpton – Westmeston – Clayton
East Chiltington – Streat – Ditchling – Keymer

So each of the twelve churches in this area features on at least one line, and Hamsey, Malling and East Chiltington feature on two. Of course it may be argued that the area is arbitrarily defined, and that extending or contracting the boundaries would change the numbers. But it is striking that all the villages along the foot of this section of the Downs have so many alignments. Also notable is that in this area one straight line links four churches, and one in the lower Cuckmere valley five churches, which does seem to have a very low probability as a random distribution.

The next cluster of churches, going westwards, is in the valley of the river Adur. The upper reaches of the river, in the Low Weald, have only two churches nearby. However the lower part, as the river completes its last eight miles to the sea through the South Downs, has twelve ancient village churches lying within two miles one side or the other. I can discern only two straight lines, viz:

Henfield – St Botolphs – Coombes
Ashurst – Steyning – Lancing

The final river valley cluster is further west around the river Arun. Again there is only a small number of churches near the upper reaches of the river, in the Weald, and no straight lines of three are in evidence. Surprisingly though, from Pulborough southwards to the sea, which is a distance of about twelve miles, there are no fewer than fifteen ancient churches within two miles of its banks, but again the same applies and no lines can be discerned.

I have looked at areas further west, and through the Weald, and in the east, but can find no lines elsewhere in the county. So the position appears to be that:

- In two localities, the lower Cuckmere valley and the springline of the Downs from Lewes to Hurstpierepoint, there are dense clusters of ancient churches with a high incidence of lines relative to the number of points (ie the number of lines is around half the number of points). Moreover in the first area five churches lie on one line, and in other four do this, which seems extraordinary.

- In the lower Adur valley, in a similar square mileage to the two areas above, there is a similar cluster of about a dozen churches but only two lines of three, which is a much lower incidence of lines compared to the number of points.

- In the lower Arun valley there is a cluster of no fewer than fifteen churches in a similar sized area but no straight lines whatsoever (though as elsewhere a few are near misses).

- Nowhere else in the county has these concentrations of churches and none yields any straight lines.

It does seem therefore that either both the first two areas by chance have alignments of churches which are very much against the odds – or there are straight lines which were a matter of design. The lines do not seem to form a pattern. Nevertheless, given the lines of four points in one area and five in the other, intention rather than chance appears to me more likely. However, if this is true it is remarkable that little or no such effort was made in the lower Adur valley (where two lines among twelve points seems much more likely to be by chance), and no alignments whatsoever can be found in the church cluster, possibly the densest in the county, in the lower Arun valley.

Why the early inhabitants of Sussex should have such wildly inconsistent practice would seem inexplicable. Also, exactly why holy places should be aligned, while much speculated on in 'new age' writing, remains a mystery.

6 THE DEVIL IN SUSSEX

The most famous feature linked with the Devil in Sussex is the Devil's Dyke – the current fashion seems to be to call it Devil's Dyke, but during my childhood in Brighton it always had the definite article and that is the usage I will follow here. The Dyke is an enormous V-shaped valley cut into the South Downs to the north of Brighton, running from the ridge of the hills down to their foot, at the village of Poynings. Its sides are so steep and even that it really does appear to have been constructed rather than eroded or otherwise formed naturally. Accordingly tradition ascribes its creation to the Devil, as recounted (among many others) by E.V. Lucas:

His punchbowl may be seen here, his footprints there; but the greatest of his enterprises was certainly the Dyke. His purpose was to submerge or silence the churches of the Weald, by digging a ditch that should let in the sea. He began one night from the North side, at Saddlescombe, and was working very

The Devil's Dyke.

well until he caught sight of the beams of a candle which an old woman had placed in her window. Being a Devil of Sussex rather than of Miltonic invention, he was not too clever, and taking the candle for the break of dawn, he fled and never resumed the labour. This is the very infirm legend that is told of the Dyke; but the great mound of earth that he flung up at Saddlescombe, so round and smooth, should help you to believe it. [37]

But discounting this legend, the real, geological formation of this huge slice almost surgically cut out of the Downs has always been a mystery to me – until now, when preparing this book. All along the upper edges of the Dyke the hillside flows in smooth curves typical of these hills, and then there is suddenly a sharp ridge, and the flat, even wall of the Dyke plunges down to the narrow gully at the bottom. The feature is described as a dry river valley, but this is problematic since rivers carve out their valleys over aeons, making them shallow, broad and irregular. Also, how can a river start flowing at the top of the Downs, when the chalk of which they are made is porous so that (as we know) rain simply soaks down in and emerges, at the bottom of the hills when it encounters harder rock? And it could not have been carved out by a glacier, since it is well known that glaciation in Britain occurred down to a line from the Thames to the Avon but not further south. On the other hand other similar, if smaller, features are observable elsewhere in the Downs (for example running southwards from Truleigh Hill, about two miles west of the Devil's Dyke) so this is clearly something that is formed when there are certain conditions, rather than being a totally unique or somehow unnatural phenomenon.

The explanation, while not being formation by a glacier, is related and stems from that same period about fourteen thousand years ago, viz:

In reality the 300-foot-deep valley was formed by tremendous amounts of water running off the Downs during the last Ice Age when large amounts of snow thawed and the frozen chalk prevented any further absorbtion; erosion was aided by the freeze-thaw cycle and the valley was deepened by the 'sludging' of the saturated chalk. [By kind permission of Brighton and Hove City Libraries] [38]

So it appears that it was a one-off cascade of melted snow, unable to soak down as the ground beneath (unlike the surface) was still frozen, and so pouring down the hillside. Presumably the flow was concentrated wherever there was a natural in-fold of the Downs, rather than where the hillside was convex, and the 'water cannon' effect quickly and evenly cut out a regular-shaped gully. This accounts for the fact that there are other examples, albeit that none rivals a depth of 300ft, and explains why the valley so carved would remain dry once the water had flowed away (presumably to the sea via existing rivers).

I suppose therefore that to include this as a 'mystery' is not strictly accurate, but I think it is a wonder whose explanation is not widely known and is therefore appropriate for inclusion. For those who prefer the explanation of the Devil, when I was growing up in Brighton an alternative to the old woman lighting a candle was that this done by St Dunstan, it being vaguely known that he had some connection with Sussex (as evidenced by the eponymous home for blind ex-servicemen and women at Ovingdean).

St Dunstan, who was Abbot of Glastonbury and then Archbishop of Canterbury in the tenth century, also features in another reported encounter with the Devil at the village of Mayfield, in the High Weald in East Sussex. E.V. Lucas again gives us an account:

According to Eadmer, who wrote one of the lives of Dunstan, that saint, when Archbishop of Canterbury, built a wooden church at Mayfield and lived in a cell hard by. St Dunstan, who was an excellent goldsmith, was one day making a chalice (or, as another version of the legend says, a horseshoe) when the Devil appeared before him. Instantly recognising his enemy, and being aware that with such a foe prompt measures alone are useful, St Dunstan at once pulled his nose with the tongs, which chanced happily to be red hot. Wrenching himself free, the Devil leaped at one bound from Mayfield to Tunbridge Wells, where, plunging his nose into the spring at the foot of the Pantiles, he "imparted to the water its chalybeate qualities", and thus made the fortune of the town as a health resort. To St Dunstan therefore, indirectly, are all the drinkers of these wells indebted."[39]

In the version that I heard when young the Devil appeared as an alluring young woman, intent on diverting Dunstan from his vow of chastity, but the saint noticed a cloven hoof protruding beneath the hem of her dress and so realised her true identity.

E.V. Lucas continues by telling us that Mayfield Palace, a retreat of the archbishops of Canterbury (which would explain Dunstan's presence there) eventually became a Roman Catholic convent school and "In the great dining-room used to be the tongs which St Dunstan used". [40]

In fact they remained there well after Lucas's book was published. In the early 1980s I was on a bank holiday day out by car with my uncle and father when we came to Mayfield, all high up and leafy with a fine main street. We parked to explore the village on foot and paused outside the open entrance of the convent school, which was attended by a nun. She invited us in to look around – I think it was an open day, and although we were not prospective parents we accepted – and not far inside the entrance there was a spacious room with a large pair of tongs affixed to one of its stone walls. She recounted the tale of St Dunstan and the Devil and identified the tongs as the very ones in the story. Whether or not they had been at the site since St Dunstan was from time to time resident there (as it appears he was) and, if so, whether the saint himself used them remains a mystery.

A strange twist to the story however is that, unknown to me at the time of the visit, my wife – who I had yet to meet – had some twelve years before had her nose tweaked with the same tongs. She had been taken to visit the school, as a prospective pupil, and her mother had confided to the mother superior that she could be a disobedient child. At this the mother superior took down the tongs from the wall and performed the 'tweaking', saying this was what they did to naughty girls. In the event my wife went to the school's sister institution a few miles away in St Leonards-on-Sea, where discipline was no less strict but enforced by less colourful means.

For those who believe the Devil might still be active today in Sussex, a key location is Chanctonbury Ring. Chanctonbury is a promontory on the ridge of the South Downs just west of the Adur valley, above the village of Steyning and about six miles north and inland from Worthing. Its 'Ring' is a copse or small wood of beech trees on the hilltop which make it a prominent landmark. I have seen it from the top of a tower block in Brighton, from Leith Hill in the Surrey sandstone hills and from further away still in the North Downs, and it can be caught sight of unexpectedly from many such places up to thirty miles away.

Chanctonbury Ring.

As often recounted , the trees were planted in his youth by Charles Goring of nearby Wiston House in the eighteenth century, and he lived long enough to see some of them approach maturity. Much earlier, the hilltop was the site of a Roman temple. Today, while the Ring has not regained the fullness of its silhouette before the great 'hurricane' of 1987, it is a considerable way towards recovery.

Tony Wales in *Sussex Ghosts and Legends* relates the tradition that you can raise the Devil by running backwards around the Ring in an anti-clockwise direction seven times on midsummer's eve. The Devil will then offer you a bowl of soup or, according to some, milk to purchase your soul. [41] Variants of this (for example on the number of circuits that must be completed, within what time, on what day, and what the Devil once raised will offer for your soul), can be seen on websites accessed on computer by entering the place name into a search engine. These sources also narrate a variety of frightening mysterious experiences on the site, some of them remarkably resembling the film 'The Blair Witch Project'. [42]

Certainly it has always struck me as a sombre, eerie and strangely silent place, despite its elevation and fine views. Somehow it is so much better at a distance, as a landmark, than it is actually to be there. But how far this is influenced by hearsay, rather than some actual phenomenon or presence (diabolical or otherwise!) is impossible to say.

7 THE MYSTERIES OF BOSHAM

Bosham's role in seventh century Sussex has already been referred to (Chapter 2, above) but it appears the village may have been significant in Roman times. The church guide [43] pictures a two- or three-times larger than life size marble head found in the parsonage garden, close to the church, in the eighteenth century. The head, whose features are to a large extent eroded, is now in the Chichester Museum (not on display at the time of writing, but due to be exhibited at the museum's Novium location in Tower Sreet, Chichester, from summer 2012). The head has been dated to the first decades of the Roman period, and we are told it was traditionally identified as depicting the Emperor Trajan (early second century) though the Emperor Nero (mid-first century) has been suggested. It appears that it is not known why such a sculpted head should have been separated from the body, or at least the neck, why the features have been so effaced or why it should have turned up in the ground at Bosham.

Bosham Church.

These are mysteries however to which Miles Russell, the specialist on Roman Sussex referred to earlier, has persuasive answers. He explains [44] that such an enormous portrait must be that of an emperor, and that while the damage to the face is extensive, enough remains of the hairstyle and features to identify the subject (from comparison with other statues) as Nero. He is also clear that what has been done to the features is deliberate damage, not natural erosion, which is of course consistent with the detachment of the head from the lower part of the statue (which must have been at least a bust, if not a full length figure). Russell relates that Nero's conduct was so appalling, even by the standards of ancient Rome, that after his death in AD 68 the senate declared a 'damnatio memoriae' in respect of him, whereby all references to and depictions of him were to be destroyed. This would explain why a giant statue of him should be dismembered, the facial features defaced almost out of recognition, and the head buried, possibly under some building. There it remained hidden, as six hundred years later Christianity was being introduced to Sussex only a few yards away.

We saw in Chapter 2 how the first person to preach Christianity to the South Saxons (albeit not successfully) was an Irish monk named Dicuill. He headed a small monastic group at Bosham when, in the year 681, St Wilfrid arrived and was given royal permission to build his minster nearby at Selsey. We do not know exactly where Dicuill's church was, but if it was on the site of the current church it is tempting to think that, with a possibly lower ground level then, it may have been the semi-submerged crypt chapel, which is a place of great stillness and sense of eternity.

How Dicuill came to be in Bosham, and how he and his followers then fared in relation to the new arrangements, is not recorded. Presumably, given Wilfrid's disdain for Celtic Christianity in its refusal to submit directly to papal authority, the Irish group would have had no part in Wilfrid's mission plan. But the only hint we have of Dicuill apart from his role at the point of Wilfrid's arrival is from place names.

A common feature in the 'Saxon' parts of England, ie the south, as distinct from the 'Angle' territories further north, is the occurrence of place names ending in the suffix '–ing' or '–ings'. Both of these are derived from the Anglo-Saxon *ingas* meaning people. [45] Hence for example in Sussex *Folca-ingas* (Fulking) is Folca's people, *Haesta-ingas* (Hastings) is Haesta's people and *Puna-ingas* (Poynings) is Puna's people. [46] Folca, Haesta and Puna seem likely to be the Anglo-Saxon clan chief or warlord founding and/or ruling the settlement.

These place names occur all over the south-east – for example Dorking, Woking and Godalming in Surrey; Barking, Epping and Mucking in Essex; Ealing in Middlesex; and Reading, Goring and Sonning in Berkshire. However, there appears to be by far the biggest concentration in Sussex, with no fewer than fifteen within a ten-mile radius of Worthing. Together with Ditchling, a few miles further east, and three others a few miles further still on the river Ouse, there is a total of nineteen in the south-centre of the county, ie the roughly 25 miles between the rivers Arun and Ouse. (There are also of course several more further east and west than this.) Why this should be is a mystery in itself. But to return to the point, the derivation of Ditchling is "Dicel-ingas",[47] and it is noticeable that the name of this founder or leader is different from the norm, in not ending in 'a', and remarkably like the Irish monk of Bosham, Dicuill. Could it be that Dicuill had earlier based his small community in the place that became Ditchling, or even that he decamped there, thirty five miles east of Wilfrid's new mission centre in Bosham, to continue his work?

We will probably never know, but this is by no means the last of the mysteries pertaining to Bosham. Another concerns one of the tombs in the church. The church guide booklet [48] relates a long-standing tradition that there was a royal palace in Bosham in King Canute's time (the early 11th century) and that his infant daughter accidentally drowned there in the millstream and was buried in the church. During work in 1865 to lower the nave floor near the chancel arch, a child's remains were found in a stone coffin identified at the time to be of the 11th century. The same place is now marked by a stone slab with the inscription:

TO THE GLORY OF GOD
AND IN MEMORY OF
A DAUGHTER OF KING CANUTE
WHO DIED EARLY IN THE 11TH CENTURY
AGED ABOUT 8 YEARS
WHOSE REMAINS LIE ENCLOSED IN A
STONE COFFIN BENEATH THIS SPOT

PLACED BY THE CHILDREN OF
THE PARISH AUGUST 1906

The church guide then relates that when further work on the floor was being undertaken in 1954 the tomb was re-opened, but this time nothing was found in the coffin except a small sealed nineteenth century bottle containing a dark brown liquid. Another booklet available in the church, by Geoffrey R. Marwood, considers these excavations in greater detail, relating that the liquid was analysed in 1954 and was believed to be putrified protein material, ie organic matter of some kind, perhaps hair or wool. Presumably this was found in the coffin in 1865 and replaced at the time in the bottle, whose seal had, however, not prevented bacterial breakdown. The bottle was returned for display in the church in 1996 [49].

An even bigger mystery than the bottle and its contents, however, is the absence in 1954 of any definite human remains, such as bones. Marwood's booklet cites the account of the 1865 excavation by the vicar, the Revd Henry Mitchell, which referred to visible remains of a child, and a newspaper report at the time saying that while the bones were reduced to dust they were clearly traceable. [50] It does seem unlikely that this dust would have been placed in a small bottle and that it would then have liquified – and had it done so, surely the 1954 analysis would have found calcium rather than just 'protein material'? But beyond this, there would seem to be no reason to disturb the skeletal outline in this way.

A further complication is that a recessed wall tomb in the north wall of the chancel bears a medieval (circa thirteenth century) effigy of a child. It might have been created as a belated memorial to King Canute's daughter. It is known to have had other locations in the church over time, [51] and it would seem to be a possibility that the bone dust was re-interred there. But if this were the case, why would the bottle containing the liquid not also be re-located there, and why would the memorial slab of 1906 (stating that the remains lay beneath) be placed over the original tomb?

Altogether the disappearing remains are a mystery. And an even greater mystery is whether they were the remains of King Canute's daughter. The evidence for this is the tradition that she was buried in the church, under the nave floor close to the chancel arch; and that when this area was excavated in 1865 a small coffin of about the right period, containing the remains of a child, were indeed found. This is persuasive but falls substantially short of being conclusive.

Another tradition is that the famous story of King Cnut's (as he is more properly called) command on the sea shore to the incoming waves to retreat, to show his sycophantic courtiers that only God had such power, happened here at Bosham. The West Sussex information website [52] refers to Bosham's long association with the story, linking it to the current liability of the village's waterfront to tidal flooding, and there are indeed signs at the harbour saying "This road floods each tide". On the April day when I last visited, a board on the quay advised that low tide was 1.8m and high tide 3.9m, a difference of around six feet – which I am told is a lot. However, a difficulty is that the story itself (regardless of location) could be apocryphal. The *Anglo-Saxon Chronicle*, which for the years following its inception in the ninth century is a contemporaneous annual record, has entries for all but three of the nineteen years of Cnut's reign, most of which record the activities of the king himself. [53] It has no reference to the incident.

Similarly, to take an example of an academic work, the Anglo-Saxon volume of the *Oxford History of England*[54] devotes twenty-three pages to Cnut's reign, but again makes no reference to the story. While another academic source (doubtless among others) *does* refer to the story, the writer indicates that it "first appears in a twelfth century history".[55] This is confirmed on a number of websites, and while this is only one century on (give or take a few years) from Cnut's time. it is probably not within living memory, which at this period must leave doubts about the authenticity of the story.

If it did occur, what is the evidence that Bosham was the location? If the tradition about a royal palace at Bosham in Cnut's time were verified, for example by archeological or documentary evidence, or even if there were confirmation that Cnut's infant daughter was buried in the church, it would make the king's presence at Bosham at some point very probable. It seems likely that only a minority of royal residences would be on the coast, so Bosham's candidacy would be strong. This would be particularly so in view of the tidal flooding to which the shoreline is prone– anyone sitting by the waves at this spot, as the tide rose, would soon demonstrate the point. In the absence of direct evidence of Cnut's presence, though, it is certainly the case that Earl Godwin, King Harold's father, was growing in prominence during Cnut's reign; and that he held the secular manor of Bosham, which was the young Harold's main home.[56] It would seem likely that at some stage he might well have

entertained the court at this residence. So, paradoxically, while the event is possibly more likely to be legendary than not, if it did occur, Bosham is probably the strongest contender for its location.

This is not the end of the mysteries of Bosham. But as the final, and greatest, one also relates to events at the furthest other edge of the county – in the east – it is considered separately in the next chapter.

8 KING HAROLD: FROM BOSHAM TO HASTINGS – AND BACK?

King Harold is linked, more than to anywhere else, with Sussex. It is notable that we know where this pivotal figure in English history grew up (in Bosham – as related in Chapter 7) and we know, or are fairly sure we know, the exact spot, at Battle, near Hastings, where he was killed. However, we do not know for certain where his body lies.

As is well known, Battle Abbey was built on the site of the battle of Hastings by command of William the Conqueror, perhaps as a monument to his victory, or to atone for the bloodshed he had caused, or some combination of the two. The twelfth century *Chronicle of Battle Abbey* reports that its founders "erected the high altar as the King had commanded, on the very place where Harold's emblem, which they call a 'standard', was seen to have fallen". [57] Nowadays a stone plaque in the open air, among the ruins of the abbey, is inscribed:

THE TRADITIONAL SITE OF
THE HIGH ALTAR OF BATTLE ABBEY
FOUNDED TO COMMEMORATE
THE VICTORY OF DUKE WILLIAM
ON 14 OCTOBER 1066
THE HIGH ALTAR WAS PLACED TO MARK
THE SPOT WHERE KING HAROLD DIED

Sadly, when I visited the site in 2010 the plaque was not chained off, and groups of French schoolchildren were ambling heedlessly across it. But it seems extremely odd that William should mark and sanctify the spot where Harold had died, possibly running a risk that it could become a shrine and centre of opposition. Perhaps he was not aware that previous English kings who had died in violent circumstances, Oswald of Northumbria and Edmund of East Anglia, had become saints and symbols of resistance to those who had killed them. However, it is consistent with Harold's depiction in the Bayeux Tapestry, where he is given the title 'Harold Rex' (king), despite his lack of royal lineage, in contrast to William himself, who is only entitled 'Dux' (duke). The implication is that Harold was not just a usurper or pretender to be treated with contempt, but someone to be accorded due respect, at least after he was safely dead. The same approach seems to apply to the question of Harold's burial. The earliest source, a poem written only a year after the battle, says that while William refused to release Harold's body to his mother, Gytha, he arranged for him to be "buried at the summit of a cliff . . . under a tombstone with the inscription "You rest here King Harold, by order of the duke, so that you may still be guardian of the shore and sea".[58]

This would presumably be somewhere on the cliffs in or around Hastings, and while it does not sound like consecrated ground, it would certainly have the potential to become hallowed ground. Alternatively, a slightly later source [59] has Harold buried at Waltham Abbey in Essex, which he had founded; and a spot, now outside the church, has a stone recording the position of the former high altar and a second stone behind it marked "Harold King of England Obiit 1066".Either of these scenarios – a not entirely respectful but public burial near Hastings, or interment behind the high altar of an abbey, would seem to be running a considerable risk. Even if a burial at Waltham had been secret, a number of people are likely to have been aware of the royal tomb, so the chance of the fact leaking out must have been quite high. It could only take a few people claiming miraculous cures at the spot to make serious trouble for the king, as Henry II was to discover a century later.

This brings us back to Bosham , where the excavation of 1954 revealed not only the stone coffin supposedly of King Cnut's daughter, but also only three feet away, and for the first time, a full sized stone coffin containing bones of an adult male. Marwood's booklet records that the magnificence of this coffin suggested an individual of very high status, and that local tradition would suggest Earl Godwin, King Harold's father (died 1053), notwithstanding the *Anglo-Saxon Chronicle* entry that he was buried at Winchester.[60] But a third booklet available in the church (which is sold with Marwood's work tucked into its inside front cover) is by local historian John Pollock,[61] and argues that the tomb and remains are those of King Harold. The church guide tells us that Bosham was among Earl Godwin's estates and that Harold's main home was there, and points out that he is pictured entering Bosham church (which is identified by name) in the Bayeux Tapestry.[62] So clearly he had a strong personal link to the village. Pollock builds on this base by:

- Arguing that the remains lack a skull and the bones of one leg, consistent with the account of Harold's death in the *Carmen de Hastingae Proelio* where, after a lance wound to the chest which probably killed him, one Norman knight beheaded him and another then severed a leg and cast it away.

- Adducing medical evidence that the fractures on the bones had not healed, meaning they were inflicted very shortly before or after death, which is consistent with the occupant of the tomb suffering multiple wounds at or after death, as did King Harold.

- In particular, establishing that the fracture on the lower part of the femur (thigh bone) which is present, the left one, is consistent with the blow to this part of Harold's left leg shown in the Bayeux Tapestry.

- Cogently arguing against some other possible high status, contemporaneous individuals being the occupant of the tomb.

- Pointing out that the tradition that 'Earl Godwin' was buried in the church, despite being recorded as buried at Winchester, could refer to Harold himself as the successor to that earldom in 1053.

- Pointing out that Bosham passed from Harold to William himself, and was the only estate in Sussex he directly retained, so that any burial in the church would be likely to be royal, and directly under his authority.

Altogether it is a persuasive argument, though ultimately circumstantial. It should be said, though, that Waltham Abbey (both the church and the town) also firmly maintains and adduces evidence for its claim to be the "last resting place of King Harold II" (as the town's 'welcome' sign has it). It is frustrating, if understandable, that in 2004 the church authorities in the Chichester diocese declined to authorise a re-excavation of the tomb of the warrior at Bosham, and of that of the child, to see whether current technology for analysing DNA (and presumably other modern scholarship) might identify both burials more conclusively. Failing this, the question remains unresolved.

One interesting postscript to this matter (at least to me) is that the vicar of Holy Trinity Church, Bosham , shown in photographs in Marwood's booklet as present at the excavations in 1954, was the Revd. Bransby A. H. Jones. By coincidence, when he was vicar of St Andrew's Church, Moulsecoomb, Brighton, he conducted the wedding of my parents and also baptised me, which gives me an unlikely personal link with this key point of history.

A final footnote is the contrasting fate of the remains of Harold's antagonist, William the Conqueror. His tomb, marked by a large incised slab, is in the Abbé des Hommes which he founded in Caen, Normandy. Information in the church, however, informs the visitor that the tomb was defiled and emptied, and that the bones were scattered by French revolutionaries and have remained lost ever since. *Sic transit gloria mundi*.

9 SAINT AND DRAGON: ST LEONARD'S FOREST

Reference has been made earlier to the lives of four saints who are commonly associated with Sussex – Wilfrid, Cuthman, Dunstan and Richard. But a fifth saint is referenced by name in the county, by way of St Leonard's Forest near Horsham, and the town of St Leonards-on-Sea next to Hastings, and when I was growing up the story of his exploits was well known. It was said that he had been a hermit living in St Leonard's Forest, and that he had slain a great dragon that had threatened and devoured travellers passing through. The existence of the hamlet of Dragon's Green in the locality was taken as a connection.

However, a documentary basis for this story was not easy to find. Initially I tracked it down in a book about British folklore, myths and legends, which relayed the story I was familiar with and added some more detail [63]. It said that the saint was wounded in the fight and wherever drops of his blood fell, lilies-of-the-valley sprang up – as witnessed by an area of the forest called the Lily Beds, about halfway between Horsham and Pease Pottage, where many of these flowers grow wild. It also said that the saint's wish that nightingales in the forest should from then on be silent, as their song had disturbed his prayers, was granted, along with his less curmudgeonly wish that adders in the forest should never again sting. Clearly these details are in the realm of legend, but what is the evidence of a real life St Leonard in Sussex, and specifically in the forest bearing his name?

A selection of standard compendia or collections of saints' lives [64,65,66,67] all list St Leonard, with a saint's day of 6th November, and then give essentially the same account. They state that there is no known reference to the saint until the eleventh century (some say c.1025), when a completely unhistorical *Vita* or life of him was published. According to this he lived in the sixth century in what is today France, and was a hermit living alone in a remote cell. One day the Frankish king Clovis was hunting in the forest, accompanied by his queen, when she went into labour and encountered difficulties. The saint intervened to ensure a safe delivery, and was rewarded by a grant of land near Limoges, where he built the abbey of Noblac (nowadays St Léonard). His cult grew rapidly from the eleventh century, and today, for example, no fewer than 177 churches in England are dedicated to him [68]. There is no mention in any of these sources of another St Leonard (apart from an eighteenth century Italian Roman Catholic priest) and so not one based in Sussex. On the other hand the element of a forest-dwelling hermit performing a notable miracle is a link. So how did the account of the Sussex dragon-slayer arise?

I can find no source for it earlier than the beginning of the twentieth century. An early nineteenth century history of the locality has no reference to the saint, although it refers to a chapel bearing a dedication to his name:

There was, before the Reformation, a chapel in the forest, of which the earliest notice that has been met with is in the taxation of Bishop Langton, in 1320, when it is excused from payment, on account of its poverty . . . In the Augmentation Office this chapel is only noticed twice. "The free chapel of St Leonard, near Horsham, no incumbent . . ." "The site is supposed to be in an inclosure (sic) of about an acre, about two miles from Horsham, near the road leading to Pease Pottage gate." [69]

For a biography of Saint Leonard of Sussex I can find only one account, published in 1922. [70] This begins when he is ten years old in the year 1056, and tending pigs in the village of Worth, which is about ten miles roughly north-east of Horsham (nowadays in Crawley). The parish priest reveals to him his true identity as a grandson of King Canute, and by virtue of lands thereby inherited at Chidham near Chichester he builds the current (late Anglo-Saxon) stone church. He becomes "head man" of the village and protects it, for example from attack by a pack of wolves and from discovery in its remote location by the new post-Conquest Norman rulers. After the village is eventually located by the authorities Leonard is returning from a visit to Chidham and encounters a dragon, which he fights and kills. It sounds like a spiritual or even a metaphorical dragon, though, as it speaks and taunts him of what, with his background, he could have achieved. He then, at around the age of forty, becomes a hermit living in a cell in the forest, which he does for the next sixty years. On his one hundredth birthday a party processes out to greet him, and finds his cell has disappeared, the spot being covered by lilies of the valley.

It can be seen that this is written as a fable or folk tale, not a biography in the academic sense. The author says, in the preface, that he does not include footnotes or references, which are "for Professors and very superior folk". Unfortunately, however, this does not allow us to know what material might have come from earlier sources (and to assess how reliable their provenance might be) and to discern what may have been embellished or created by the writer.

We can be sure, however, that he did not completely invent the story, and that his book was based on some previous narrative of a St Leonard in the area, because there is a reference dating from twenty years earlier. In his book *The Four Men,* Hilaire Belloc records himself explaining to his companions, in St. Leonard's Forest, that the saint lived there in a little hermitage, that he was born and drank ale in the area, and that he never left other than once to go to Germany to convert the heathen there. [71]

It seems likely that Belloc would have had some source for this but what it was remains a mystery.

Another puzzle surrounds Worth Church (dedication St Nicholas) whose construction A.C. Crookshank is undoubtedly right to date to the late Anglo-Saxon period. Local archaeologist Richard Symonds has pointed out to me that it is a very fine and large church for the tiny community recorded in Domesday Book, both at the time (1086) and some decades before, under King Edward the Confessor. [72] He believes that its foundation by a saint may account for this, and certainly a church catering for pilgrims would be larger (and better financed) than the parish church of a remote hamlet. However, there is no documentary or archeological evidence for this, and it seems possible there could be other reasons for a church to be larger than might be expected.

It is striking however that the church's thirteenth century font has a most remarkable motif on its northern side, a horizontally double cross of which I

The font in Worth Church.

have never seen anything similar elsewhere. It is reproduced on the font cover and on an altar cloth and a plaque elsewhere in the building, so as to have become a kind of symbol for the church. Although in single form this cross is not uncommon as a heraldic device this does not appear to be the case for the double version. It also seems unlikely that a lord or noble would place an emblem of his worldly authority on a font, the entry point to membership of the universal church. Is it remotely possible that it could have been devised as St Leonard's cross?

Be that as it may, my theory about St. Leonard of Sussex, which I put forward very tentatively, is as follows. Whatever the truth about St. Leonard of Limoges, the publication of his *Life* around the year 1025 clearly created a rapidly-growing cult in Europe, including in England. It appears likely to me that the chapel in the forest near Horsham that was in existence by 1320 (and possibly well before), with a dedication to St. Leonard, was part of this process and that the dedication was in fact to the sixth century hermit of Noblac. Because he had lived in a cell in a forest, at some stage local people started to think the setting for his life had been the eponymous chapel in their forest, not the one in the area of Limoges.

As a variant on this, it is possible that the chapel in St. Leonard's forest contained or was a cell for an anchorite, and that at some stage people started to merge him in their minds with the saint to whom the chapel was dedicated. He may even, like Julian of Norwich, have adopted the name of the saint pertaining to the church in which he was confined. In this sense there may have been a St. Leonard of Sussex, beatified by popular consensus (like early saints such as Cuthman) rather than formal canonisation at Rome (of which there is no evidence).

The existence of a real figure has a little support from the size (and expensive stone construction) of the church at the tiny nearby settlement of Worth; and by the detail given of his parentage, and his descent from King Cnut, which would seem a pointless fact to invent. However, at the end of the day we cannot be certain whether or not St. Leonard of Sussex is a historical figure. (Having said that, of course, the existence of St. Leonard of Limoges is solely reliant on a *Life* of c.1025 which all modern sources agree is completely unhistorical!)

But where would the dragon come from? It is the case that the neighbouring woodland of Tilgate Forest has the preserved footprint of a dinosaur, [73] and it may be that tales of dragons in general arose from discoveries of their bones before the dawn of scientific archaeology. It is notable that the pub at Dragon's Green is called the George and Dragon, so it may well be that the place has no allusion to St Leonard but merely grew up round an inn (like many others) named in honour of England's patron saint.

However, this was not the end of mythical beasts in the area. A history from the early nineteenth century (among other sources) refers to and quotes from a seventeenth century document as follows:

The tradition is that there was formerly a dragon in this forest is occasioned by a book, entitled "True and wonderful! A discourse relating to a true and monstrous serpent (or dragon) lately discovered and yet living, to the great annoyance and divers slaughters both of men and cattell, by his strong and violent poyson: in Sussex, two miles from Horsham, in a woode called St Leonard's Forest, and thirty miles from London, this present month of August, 1614. With the true generation of serpents. Printed at London, by John Trundle, 1614." In which he is thus described: "This monster was above 9 feet long, shaped like an axle tree, with bunches at his side like footballs, which they feared might turn to wings, he casts his venom 4 rods, and his principal food is the rabbits of a neighbouring warren; it had been seen by the Horsham carrier, and other three, who attest this account". It was probably a satire on some obnoxious proprietor. [74]

This last theory is only one of a number of speculations about how the account arose. E.V. Lucas gives a longer quotation from the original account, concluding with its signatories "John Steele, Christopher Holder, And a Widow Woman dwelling nere Faygate", and wonders what it was they really saw. He observes that it "must have had a basis of some kind",[75] implying a belief that its origin was some real phenomenon rather than a satire.

It has been suggested to me that it could have been a story made up to scare people away from the forest by someone engaged in illegal activity there, such as smuggling. The difficulty with this though is that it could clearly be equally likely to provoke an armed search party, which would be the opposite of what was wanted.

An author in the 1960s, Sheila Kaye-Smith, considered that the account had been written with more attention to detail and less sensationalism than would be the case if it were just an invention or drunken delusion. She surmised that the most likely explanation was a large non-native snake, which could approach the proportions given, and might have originated as an escapee from a private menagerie, perhaps gathered by someone who had travelled abroad. [76]

Certainly the creature as described lacks the wings and claws of a 'dragon' and appears much more akin to a 'serpent' or snake. It is notable that whereas its victims start out in the extended title as "men and cattell", they subsequently come down, in the more detailed content, to rabbits, which would be a normal diet for a large constrictor. As Kaye-Smith observed, the lumps on the side of the creature sound less like embryonic wings (the conclusion the authors jumped to) than a meal such as a rabbit being digested. [76] And since the snakes familiar to the witnesses would not have been large constrictors but adders, which are much smaller but poisonous snakes, the venom could be a natural fearful assumption rather than something actually technically witnessed.

So the theory of a large constrictor, imported perhaps when younger and much smaller, and escaped when grown to adult proportions, seems to me the most likely explanation. Given that this would have been a very much larger snake than any the witnesses were familiar with, together with the existing tradition of a dragon in the forest, it is possible to see how the account might have arisen. But this is not known for sure, and the matter remains open and unresolved.

A final postscript takes us back to St Leonard. As noted above, he is also referenced in Sussex by the town of St. Leonards-on-Sea, which stands on the coast next to Hastings and now forms part of that borough. It was built on undeveloped land in the 1820s as a 'new town' seaside resort by a London builder, James Burton. [77] In the middle ages there had been a parish of St. Leonard corresponding to the site, but its church – on a spot now in Norman Road in the town – disappeared from records after the early fifteenth century.[78] It appears therefore that the town and its early Victorian parish church of St. Leonard (now re-built after destruction by a V1 flying bomb in 1944) were named from the dedication of the former medieval church. There is thus no suggestion of any presence by a St. Leonard (whether of Sussex or Limoges) in the area at any time. It is an odd coincidence, though, that in both cases (St. Leonard's Forest and St. Leonards-on-Sea) the original medieval church dedicated to the saint has utterly disappeared.

10 THE ANSTY CROSS

The hamlet of Ansty lies pretty well in the centre of Sussex, about halfway between both the county's eastern and western borders, and its northern border and the sea. Its most noticeable feature, to anyone passing through, is its pub 'The Ansty Cross', and in particular – until spring 2011 – the pub's very striking sign. It showed a white cross on a black background. The cross's shape (see figure 1) had arms of equal length, tapering out very slightly (though not as much as a Maltese cross) with a finial at the end of each arm like a fleur-de-lys. Between each finial and the next one there was an arc, almost a quarter of a circle, so that the cross had a broken circle around its edge. It was a design of cross that I had never seen elsewhere, and in recent years (while visiting the area regularly for family reasons) I began to wonder whether it could be possible that Ansty had its own unique cross, like Canterbury, Winchester or St Albans. However, it is obviously not a great centre of pilgrimage as they are. Also, on consideration, the basis for the pub's name seemed more likely to be its position: although it lies at a T-junction of the east-west A272 and a road going southwards to Burgess Hill, there is a small lane northwards a short way away, and the spot could arguably be referred to as a crossroads.

Figure 1   Figure 2   Figure 3

The situation is further complicated by the existence, on the pub's front gable, of a similar but not identical cross (see figure 2). The most noticeable difference is that it lacks an encirclement, and (it later turned out, significantly) is coloured green. When I happened to visit the pub in 2009 I asked the staff if anyone knew where either cross design came from, but none of them knew their origins or any significance. The hamlet has what appears to have been a small twentieth century church, which might, as so often elsewhere, have contained a lead, but it is now a private residence. I started to feel on the one hand that the lack of any explanation for these similar, and unusual, cross designs attaching to the pub, was intriguing. On the other hand I guessed that the most likely explanation was merely that 'The Ansty Cross' referred to the road junction, and that two similar designs to illustrate the name had been chosen on the whim of a previous landlord or brewery.

I learned, however, that Ansty lies in the parish of its larger neighbour, Cuckfield, so while walking in the area more recently I called in to see if its church guide might make any reference. It did not, but I noticed for the first time that the tower of the church featured a metal cross, in fact a 'wall tie plate' to support the structure, of once again a similar but slightly different design (see figure 3). This has arms of equal length but they do not taper, and a finial at each end which is almost a fleur-de-lys but lacks the central 'prong' (of the three that would normally feature).

I was even more struck to notice that at the other end of the village a building, once a free church chapel, had two metal wall tie plates on its front wall of exactly the same design (again figure 3). It was beginning to get very confusing – was there a Cuckfield cross related to but different from an Ansty one, or were they variants from one origin, or was it all just coincidence?

It occurred to me that a very possible explanation was that the origin of one or more of the crosses might be heraldic rather than ecclesiastical, ie a motif drawn from the coat of arms of a local landowner or otherwise prominent family. The most likely candidates could be the families that owned or had owned extensive estates in different parts of Sussex, to my knowledge the Fitzalans, Howards, Nevills or Pelhams; or those who had been 'big fish' just in the locality. Judging from the number of memorial monuments in Cuckfield parish church these were most likely to be the Burrell, Sergison, Hendley or Bowyer families. A check on various websites that depict coats of arms that they advise are associated with different surnames yielded illustrations for all these names, mostly consistently between websites, with none featuring anything resembling the crosses at Ansty or Cuckfield.

A further dead end was that none of the websites I visited illustrating the many different designs of cross that exist showed the pub sign one with its surrounding circle (figure 1) or the wall tie plate one at Cuckfield (figure 3), though it transpired that the cross on the pub gable is a recognised design known as a *cross patonce*.

I next wrote to the landlord or manager of the Ansty Cross pub to ask whether he or she could shed any light, but on passing the pub a week or two later noticed that it had closed! It seemed that I was fated to draw a blank on even determining whether this was a mystery, or whether it was just a phantom of my own, by now slightly obsessive, imagination.

Help came in an e-mail from the parish archivist at Cuckfield, in response to the query I had sent to the vicar. I was very grateful for his kindness in spending time on this at all. He said that he and the church architect were "in agreement that the wall plates are not heraldic, but a local blacksmith doing an excellent job in making plates that are a little more decorative than normal." He continued that ". . . the Ansty Cross . . . was originally the Green Cross at Ansty, the green cross referring to a local family coat of arms – I think the Hendley's, but I am not absolutely certain. However that cross had a longer vertical than horizontal element . . ." [79]

So there had been a green cross associated with Ansty, hence the colour of the cross on the pub gable; and it had originated from a local coat of arms, though possibly the original had been longer vertically than horizontally, unlike the pub gable symbol. Further confirmation came from my discovering a row of houses in Ansty called Green Cross Cottages. However, I knew from earlier research that it was not the arms of the Hendley family.

However, the local history section of Brighton public library came to the rescue. *A History of the Parish of Cuckfield* which was nearly a century old said:

"It would be no less interesting to trace at length the generations of the Hussey family. Though they have left no mark behind them to-day except their heraldic sign, the green cross, which is still conspicuous at Ansty, they were important figures in Cuckfield when they lived at Pain's Place and Leighs or Little Ease. But their chief claim to note lay in their parliamentary services to Sussex which lie outside a strictly parochial history. As early as 1289 one Henricus Husee was summoned to Edward I's parliament to represent Sussex, and he was returned continuously through eight more parliaments until 1340, by which time the county must have been represented by the Father of the House. In 1400 and 1402 another Henricus Husee was returned for the county......In 1552 'Sir Henry Hussey, Knt., was returned for Horsham.....In 1558 Anthonius Hussey, armiger, sat for Shoreham." [80]

The account continues by relating that "the family seems to have become scattered" after 1621, and that they had disappeared from local history by the end of the seventeenth century.[81] Apart, of course, from their green cross.

However, there then occurred another twist in this convoluted pursuit. The section on Cuckfield in a website called *British History Online* [82] gave a black-and-white illustration of the local Hussey coat of arms, described as 'Barry ermine and gules', which featured no cross – and evidently no green (since this is *vert* in heraldic terminology, derived from French). But the section also illustrated a coat of arms relating to the name Ward, which family it said held the local manor of Bolnore in the late eighteenth to early nineteenth century – and this comprised just a plain cross patonce on a shield. However the arms are described as 'Azure a cross paty or'. Since *azure* and *or* mean blue and gold respectively, the cross is clearly not green.

Having sent a query at an earlier stage to the College of Arms in London, but with insufficient information to enable them to help, I was able to write back with these further details. One of their heralds (as their experts are termed) kindly advised me as follows:

"Several Hussey families had a simple green cross on a gold shield...and not surprisingly in the days of unregulated heraldry . . ...other families called Hussey adopted the same or similar arms . . .

I suspect it's simply a case of the plain green cross being given a bit of ad-hoc ornamentation when taken out of its heraldic context; it may have become patonce in stages . . .

The Hendleys of Cuckfield do not appear to have used arms with any kind of cross in them; the principal element in their arms was the martlet . . .

The General Armory [83] *does not list any armigerous Wards in Sussex, though a Surrey family of the name is ascribed a cross pattée (ie paty or formy)"* [84]

Unless I required further searching, this advice was offered without charge, for which I was very grateful and would like to express thanks here. It seemed to me that a point had been reached where there was a good deal of light shed on the mystery, and that further inquiries would be subject to the law of diminishing returns. In summary it could fairly reliably be concluded that:

• The Hussey family, who lived close to Ansty and provided Sussex MPs from the thirteenth to the sixteenth century, had a plain green cross on a gold background as their coat of arms.

• This became a symbol within, and/or of, the area, perhaps as a marking on properties owned by the family and let out to tenants.

• It 'morphed' into a *cross patonce* as shown on the pub gable, either through an evolution towards a more ornamental form, or by confusion with the *cross patonce* of a different colour on another local coat of arms, that of the Wards (notwithstanding the absence of any arms-bearing Sussex Wards in *Burke's General Armory* [83]).

• The cross was further developed into the one on the pub sign, with a bordering circle slightly reminiscent of a celtic cross, by the creator or commissioner of the sign – making what is, for me, one of the most striking and pleasing crosses to be seen.

Further evidence to back these conclusions came from accidentally coming across a book on heraldry in Sussex while researching another chapter of this book at Hastings library. This said, notwithstanding the absence of any "armigerous Wards in Sussex" [81] in *Burke's General Armory*, that the arms of the Wards of Cuckfield were "Azure, a cross patonce or" i.e. a gold *cross patonce* on a blue background [85].

The very final twist was that in spring 2011 the pub sign which had originally sparked my interest was removed, this being some months after the closure of the pub as noted above. But across the road a village sign went up at about the same time, comprising what looks like a coat of arms. In the half towards the viewer's right hand is a deer with a bush above and behind it; while in the left hand half is a green *cross patonce* (longer vertically than horizontally) on a gold background. This would appear to be the Hussey coat of arms, either as it actually was, or with a plain green cross having become patonce by ornamentation or by fusion with the Ward heraldic cross.

It occurred to me that the new village sign must have been put up by a local authority, most likely the parish council (ie not the ecclesiastical parish, but the most basic level of local government). While such a body would normally be confined to ensuring the mowing of grass verges etc, and could not be expected to be expert in the history of the locality, I thought they might be aware of the origin of a sign they had just put up. So I wrote to the clerk of Ansty and Staplefield Parish Council with this query. She kindly replied clarifying that the sign replaced an earlier worn and weathered version, and forwarding advice from a contact (I inferred the sign's painter), saying:

The green cross comes from the shield on the coat of arms of the HUSSEY family, who were land owners in Ansty. They owned the Harvest Hill estate, including the site of the former pub, known as The Green Cross until about 1980, when it was renamed The Ansty Cross. A green cross can still be seen on the front of this building. [86]

So the distinctive 'Ansty Cross' is now confirmed as a green cross from the Hussey coat of arms, with its *patonce* shape perhaps derived later, possibly from the Ward coat of arms. The elongated nature (from top to bottom) of the version on the village sign could be because it is confined to the left hand side of the shield, which is only half as wide as its height, whereas to fill a full shield the cross would naturally have more equal dimensions.

I was ready to conclude also that the metal wall crosses at Cuckfield on the parish church tower, and on the former chapel, which have a structural rather than decorative function, probably were the separate design of the local blacksmith who would have made them. I thought it possible though that he was influenced by the similar crosses on the pub at Ansty. However, considerable doubt was cast on this by an unlikely coincidence. While researching for the next chapter of this book, which involved a visit to the site of a Civil War skirmish at Greatham Bridge on the river Arun, I ended my walk at the village of Amberley. One cottage there bore a metal wall tie plate identical to the ones in Cuckfield, some twenty five miles away. If the crosses at Cuckfield were made by a local blacksmith, which had seemed likely, then he had a remarkably wide sales area. Or it could have been one blacksmith copying another; or one metalwork company in mass production.

The doubt was compounded by my noticing, again by chance, when looking through *Burke's General Armory* [81] because of my referral to it regarding the Husseys, that the Cuckfield metal cross is actually one of twenty-eight cross designs commonly used in heraldry. It is known as a *cross moline* and therefore could be drawn from a coat of arms, though given its appearance at Amberley as well as Cuckfield it would be difficult to know where to start looking. I decided that having found the root of the Ansty cross in the Hussey family, the origin of the *cross moline* as a design of wall tie plate could remain a mystery . . .

To complicate matters, however, I discovered still later that the distinctive thirteenth century cross carved on the font in Worth church (see illustration on page 48) is a double version of this very same cross. This (so far as I can tell) unique symbol means, I think, that we can talk of the Worth Cross as well as the Ansty Cross, and be possibly more confident of an origin in faith rather than heraldry.

11 THE BATTLE OF WEST HOATHLY

One of the most beautiful and tranquil spots in Sussex must surely be West Hoathly. The village stands 600ft up on the ridge of the High Weald, the wooded and shady churchyard spreading south from the church and then suddenly dropping down by terraces into a deep valley. At the point where this descent begins there is a seat from which the visitor can admire the view southwards across the weald and towards the South Downs, some fifteen miles away. Set in the wall behind the seat there has been, ever since I can remember, a stone inscribed with the lines:

> *Friend, looking out on this wide Sussex view,*
> *Know they who rest here looked and loved it too:*
> *Pray then like them to sleep, life's labour past,*
> *In your remembered fields of home at last.*

But there is evidence in this peaceful place of a dramatically violent past. In the church there is a simple and tiny brass tablet memorial to Anne Tree, a villager who was a Protestant martyr burned to death for her faith in nearby East Grinstead in 1556. More recently, when I was young, the graves of two Second World War German bomber crew members lay on the southern edge of the churchyard, at the bottom of the valley, their aircraft having crash landed locally. The graves are no longer there, and I have been told that the remains were at some point repatriated to Germany.

But the mysterious conflict, if there was one, dates from the seventeenth century. The great wooden door of the church has a date (it appears likely its date of origin) in large letters consisting of iron studs, MARCH 31 1626. The door also features, focused around its upper right hand side, half a dozen semi-globular indentations. They vary a little in size but none are very far from about a half to three-quarters of an inch across and up to about half an inch deep. Like the surface of the door around them, they are smoothed and shiny with age. When I first visited, as a child, my father told me that they were musket ball holes made by Parliamentarian soldiers in the English Civil War, firing as Royalist soldiers retreated into the church slamming the door behind them. He said he had been told this a few years earlier by the landlord of the Cat Inn in the village, while taking refreshment there. The church guide [87] describes the door, but makes no mention of the holes; though an earlier version (1976) briefly stated that they were said to have been made during a local skirmish between Cavaliers and Roundheads. When I visited sometime around 2005, a member of the congregation who was working in the church said she knew of the story but could add nothing more, and did not believe that anything further was known. She did put me in touch with the church archivist, who was, however, able to confirm only the same picture.

So, what is the likelihood of an engagement at West Hoathly in the English Civil War? To consider this, it is helpful to look briefly at the wider context.

As is well known, the immediate origin of the war was Parliament's strengthening grip on London in its dispute with King Charles I, leading to the king's decision to depart in 1642. In August that year he raised his standard at Nottingham [88] and by the end of the year established his headquarters nearer still, about 60 miles from the capital, at Oxford.[89] A series of maps in one current source on the war [90] shows Parliamentarian territory by spring 1643 as including all of southern England except Cornwall, and much of eastern England up to Hull, so that Oxford was very much a forward Royalist position – and the nearest point of the front line to Sussex. However, by autumn 1643 the south-west had fallen to the Royalists, leaving the front line (in the south) as a line from Oxford to Southampton, at nearest about 20 miles west of any point in Sussex. This remained the case in autumn 1644, notwithstanding Parliament's big territorial gains in the midlands and north at that stage, which eventually led to its victory in 1646.

It is evident, though, that in practice the boundary was much more porous and fluid than this, with various enclaves and numerous forays on both sides into each other's territory. Firstly, at the very beginning of the war, in late 1642, a Royalist army entered Sussex, captured Chichester and advanced thirty miles east to Cuckfield. On leaving the village however they were engaged at Haywards Heath (at that time a heath, not a town) by a Parliamentarian force, and were defeated and scattered. [91] West Hoathly lies about six miles north-west of Haywards Heath, so a satellite skirmish there would not be beyond possibility.

As noted above, Parliamentarian domination of the south of England followed, but then the Royalists gradually took control of the south-west, including much of Hampshire, by autumn 1643. It is clear that an advance into Sussex was then undertaken. First Arundel Castle, at a crossing on the river Arun about fourteen miles into Sussex from the boundary with Hampshire, fell to the Royalists on 9 December 1643. It was however besieged on 19 December by a Parliamentarian army under General Sir William Waller, and was recaptured by them on 6th January 1644.[92]

About six miles north of Arundel there is a small village called Greatham, and the guide to its church [93] says that in the 1950s the remains of five men were found buried, without coffins, by its north wall. They are believed to have been soldiers killed in a Civil War skirmish at Greatham Bridge, a medieval structure which still spans the river Arun about a mile from the village. An engagement is evidenced by cannon balls of the period which have been found at the bridge. Nothing more appears to be known, but it seems likely it was a Royalist attempt to cross the Arun so as to proceed eastwards, and it is possible that this was contemporary with the similar action a little downstream at Arundel.

Certainly, at exactly the same time as the conflict at Arundel another engagement was taking place a dozen miles east, ie further into Sussex, on the river Adur. E.V. Lucas records the following letter from a John Coulton to a Samuel Jeake of Rye dated 8 January 1644:

The enemy attempted Bramber Bridge, but our brave Carleton and Evernden with his Dragoons and our Coll.'s horses welcomed them with drakes and muskets, sending some 8 or 9 men to hell (I feare) and one trooper to Arundel Castle prisoner, and one of Captain Evernden's Dragoons to heaven.[94]

The correspondents sound like Puritan sympathisers, and, as indicated above, by 8 January Arundel Castle was just back in Parliamentarian hands, so a prisoner sent there would be a Royalist. If so, this records a successful resistance to Royalists trying to push eastwards at a key point, a bridge over the river Adur.

West Hoathly is about twenty miles or so further north than these places, but only about ten miles further east than Bramber. An engagement at West Hoathly in late 1643 or early 1644, when Royalist forces were trying to press eastwards from Hampshire, would therefore seem to be very possible.

Intriguingly, though, if the holes date from an earlier skirmish in late 1642 (linked to the battle at Haywards Heath at that time) they would be contemporary with the indecisive battle of Turnham Green in December that year. This is at a site west of London, but so close that today it has an underground station! An engagement at West Hoathly at the same time would have been part of the high water mark of the royalist campaign, when, had they persisted, they might have closed in on London from two directions and reduced the parliamentary territory to just the eastern seaboard.

Be that as it may, it is difficult to see what else might have caused the rounded indentations in the door other than musket balls : certainly musket shot on sale in an antiques market in Arundel in 2011 were about the right size. On a recent visit to the village a local resident told me she thought the holes might stem from a shotgun wedding wherein the weapon had actually been discharged (!)

but it seems unlikely that such a dramatic event would not have left an available record. Conversely it would be completely understandable that after the Restoration the village would not trumpet its setting as the scene of a royalist rout (if that is what happened), and even after the Stuarts were later ousted the established church would be unlikely to commemorate a puritan victory.

It is impossible, too, to think of any other conflict between the age of the longbow and the age of the rifle in which an armed exchange might have happened. We also know that the door was in existence at this time from the (very fortuitous) date on it. On the other hand we cannot be absolutely sure of a Civil War engagement, and the details and outcome of the incident, assuming it happened, remain unknown.

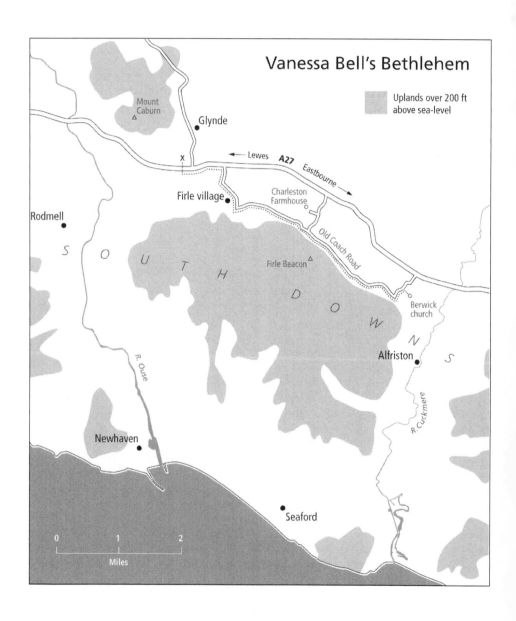

Vanessa Bell's Bethlehem

Uplands over 200 ft
above sea-level

Mount
Caburn

Glynde

Lewes **A27** Eastbourne

X

Firle village

Charleston
Farmhouse

Rodmell

S O U T H

Firle Beacon

D O

Old Coach Road

W

Berwick
church

N

R. Ouse

Alfriston

S

R. Cuckmere

Newhaven

Seaford

0   1   2

Miles

12 VANESSA BELL'S BETHLEHEM

For our final mystery we return to the Cuckmere valley, which as we have seen is an area rich in ancient enigmas and an 'other worldly' atmosphere. But this mystery is a modern one, at least in the sense that it dates from just within living memory.

As is well known, in the inter-war years the 'Bloomsbury group' of progressive intellectuals included the writers Leonard and Virginia Woolf, Lytton Strachey, E.M. Forster and Vita Sackville-West, the art critic Roger Fry, the great economist John Maynard Keynes and the painters Vanessa Bell and Duncan Grant. [95] The Woolfs famously had a country cottage in Sussex at the village of Rodmell, in the valley of the river Ouse as it passes through the South Downs, where they often played host to the others. Similarly Vanessa Bell (who was Virginia Woolf's sister), her partner Duncan Grant and her son Quentin Bell had a country base at Charleston Farmhouse, about seven miles away just north of the South Downs, between the Ouse and Cuckmere valleys. [96] Charleston Farmhouse may be visited today and is a museum containing many examples of their beautifully coloured and powerful works of decorative and other art.

Early in the second world war the bishop of Chichester was the left-leaning George Bell (no relation to Vanessa or her husband, Clive Bell). He believed in forging links between the church and the arts and proposed that the adornment of medieval churches with murals or wall paintings, which had survived the Reformation in only a few places in Sussex (notably Clayton, Hardham and Coombes) should be revived by modern artists. His attention was drawn to the early Modernist art of Duncan Grant, and it was agreed that Berwick church – a victim of heavy-handed Victorian restoration, and close to Charleston – would be the place to put the aspiration into practice.

Notwithstanding the unconventional nature of the household at Charleston, which if apprehended would surely have been disapproved of at the time (and especially in church circles), Bell and Grant were commissioned to do the work.[97] The paintings were actually executed on large boards, subsequently brought to the church and fitted closely to the wall space;[98] but it is not clear whether this was to avoid disruption of services while the work was proceeding, or to facilitate removal if the work proved unpopular. Perhaps it was a bit of both. However the work– the initial part of which was carried out in 1941–42 – was widely acclaimed.

As such, further paintings were added by Quentin Bell and Duncan Grant in 1943–44.[99] The whole ensemble makes Berwick to this day the object of pilgrimage on both religious and artistic grounds. Curiously, however, the achievement clearly did not start a trend in Sussex (or really elsewhere) as Bishop Bell seems to have envisaged. Perhaps Berwick was unusual in that the plain leaded lights in its nave did not have figures or colour to clash with the paintings around them, and this was even more pronounced after bomb damage caused them to be replaced with completely plain glass.[100] This gives beautiful views of the surrounding Sussex countryside, which seem to complement rather than compete with the paintings, many of which have the same countryside as their background.

The six larger works are *Christ in Glory* and a crucifixion scene, *The Victory of Calvary*, by Duncan Grant; *The Supper at Emmaus* and *The Wise and Foolish Virgins* by Quentin Bell; and *The Annunciation* and *The Nativity* by Vanessa Bell. The last two contrast in that *The Annunciation* (albeit set at Charleston's walled garden [101]) has, to me, a sunny Italian atmosphere and pastel shades reminiscent of Fra Angelico; while *The Nativity* has a background and quality of light which place it firmly in Sussex. While all six paintings are compelling, the finest in my opinion is *The Nativity*. It is a traditional nativity with the holy

Vanessa Bell's nativity scene in the church at Berwick.

family flanked by shepherds and animals, but the former are by their dress and 'Pyecombe' crooks unmistakeably contemporary Sussex shepherds. The note on a greetings card on sale in the church tells us the 'stable' is a Sussex barn, which in the painting has a large opening or space rather than a wall behind the figures, through which a green hill can be seen against the sky. From the viewer's perspective the hill has a gentle upward gradient from left to right, then rises more sharply to the summit, and then starts very gradually to decline away to the right.

What seized me a few years ago was that the greetings card mentioned above, depicting the painting, described the hill as being either Firle Beacon or Mount Caburn. Both of them are prominent peaks in the South Downs, respectively about three miles and about six miles west-north-west of Berwick. I decided to try to find out which of the two it might be, and then with reference to the hill to identify the actual place where the foreground of the painting was set.

As it happens their direction from Berwick is initially followed by a major track running along the bottom of the Downs, signposted as the 'old coach road' and heading roughly westward towards Firle village. (*See map on page 62.*) So I set out to walk this route, with the Downs to my left, towards the bottoms of the two hills in question. Firle Beacon, being the nearer of the two, was in view right from the start – but from the direction of Berwick its profile was a mirror image of the hill in the painting. Clearly then if Firle Beacon is the one depicted it must be as viewed when coming from the opposite direction.

After three miles I reached Firle Beacon, which stood above me to my left as I was going westwards. As I skirted its lower slopes Mount Caburn came into view, about three miles ahead and, excitingly, exactly matching the shape of the hill in the painting. On looking at the map, I was even more struck to see that the spot (OS grid ref. 067/487) was where the track ran along the southern boundary of Charleston Farm. I immediately imagined the artist with her sketchpad or easel coming out from the house and settling at this spot, to draw the view westwards for the very purpose of the painting.

However, the question was not to be so conveniently solved. Caburn from this point was very much smaller, ie further away, than the hill is in relation to the foreground figures in the painting. If the hill depicted is Caburn it is captured from this direction, certainly, but from a closer viewpoint. I therefore drew a straight line on the map from the point concerned to the summit of Caburn, and tried to keep as close to it as possible as I headed forward. It is not possible to keep Caburn in view at all times, due to intervening landscape features and dips in ground level, but recurrent sightings showed it growing closer to the apparent size, and hence distance behind the foreground figures, in the painting.

As I walked I also looked backwards towards Firle Beacon. When I was just over half a mile past it, it clearly also matched the shape of the hill in the painting, but was much too close. Beyond that point however the land falls away as you proceed westwards, ie you are going downhill towards Firle village, so that the mature woodland around the base of the Beacon blocks any sight of it. It is not until you emerge beyond Firle village, turn left and westward along the main A27 (Lewes–Eastbourne) road for a short way, and then turn right up the minor road towards Glynde, that you gain altitude so that it reappears. However by now it is about 1¾ miles distant and too small to match the hill in the painting.

It is possible to get a sight of Firle Beacon at about the right distance, which I judge to be about 1–1¼ miles, by moving south off the track to go up the lower slopes of the Downs, or north off the track by entering Firle Park. However, both views are still partially obscured by trees, and neither view is then from quite the angle shown in the painting.

So, what of Caburn? It is intermittently visible from just before Firle village, and then again just after. Following the road out of the village, after half a mile it joins the main A27 (Lewes–Eastbourne) road. If you then turn left and westward along this main road for a short way, and then turn right to take the minor road up towards Glynde, at this junction (OS grid ref. 082/463) Caburn appears to the north-west framed by the open entrance to a field. In my estimation this matches the view of the hill in the *Nativity* painting in terms of size/distance (the map shows the peak is just over a mile distant).

Two other things are apparent from this spot. Firstly, the wooded patch on the facing hillside of Caburn, which is now clearly visible, broadly matches that shown in the painting. (The similar woodland on the facing hillside of Firle Beacon, when seen from half a mile and again 1¾ miles to its west, is noticeably more a vertical line than a patch). Secondly, to the left of Caburn (as seen by the viewer) there is the distant horizontal line of the South Downs as they resume the other side of the river Ouse. There is no such feature when viewing Firle Beacon from its west. The painting shows a faint horizontal streak here which I had always assumed to be dark cloud. However, closer examination in the church shows it to be grey-green rather than the turquoise I had perceived it to be, suggesting downland not cloud.

The question arises though that, if the hill is Caburn, why should it be selected as the background? Obviously the intention was to place the scene locally, but why this particular choice? As noted above, the paintings were undertaken in 1941–42, and it happened that this was around the time, or shortly after, Virginia Woolf took her own life in March 1941.[102] Virginia had delighted in the view from her garden of Caburn, [103] which from Rodmell lay to the north up the Ouse valley; and if or when Vanessa became aware that it could also be seen looking west from the perimeter of Charleston it might have been thought of as a link between them. It must be the only feature that can be seen from both places. Also the viewpoint, from the turning off the A27 towards Glynde, is only a little over half a mile from Virginia Woolf's first house in Sussex (before she had met Leonard) which lay at the north end of Firle village. [104] As such, it is moving to think that Vanessa Bell's depiction of Caburn in *The Nativity*, from this location, might have been in memory and honour of her sister.

After all this exhaustive (and exhausting) effort to identify the hill in the painting as Caburn not Firle, I discovered that the church guide – in contrast to the greetings card, which is still on sale and citing both hills – identifies it only as Caburn! [105] However, the guide sheds no more light than the greetings card on where Caburn is painted from, and hence where the nativity scene is set.

I believe I have identified this spot. It remains intriguing, though, that the very first appearance of Caburn from this direction is from 'the old coach road' three miles away as it runs along the southern boundary of Charleston Farm. Could Vanessa Bell not have sketched it from this point and simply enlarged it? This is obviously possible, though I think she would have to have photographed it with a zoom lens, or looked at it through binoculars, to see (and depict) so clearly the shape of the woodland on its facing slope, and the horizontal line to the left of the continuing South Downs beyond.

The author's friend Bob Sinclair with Caburn behind. Compare with the illustration on page 64.

My best guess is that the sight of Caburn from the proximity of Charleston may have suggested to the artist a fitting background, but that she sketched it from the same direction but much closer – from the turning off the A27 towards Glynde. It may be by the din and roar of traffic on the A27, but it looks outward and upward to the serene and lofty peak of Caburn. If I am right, this is Vanessa Bell's Bethlehem and, in some kind of way, the Bethlehem of Sussex.

REFERENCES

(1) Zosimus, *New History*, IV, trans. Ronald T. Ridley, Australian Association for Byzantine Studies, 1982.

(2) ibid.

(3) Procopius, *Bellum Vandalicum*, trans. H.B Dewing, S. Heineman, 1914.

(4) *The Book of Armagh*, ed. John Gwynn , Ch. VII, Part VI, *The Confession of St Patrick*, p. lxxxi, Hodges,Figgis & Co. Ltd, Dublin 1908.

(5) Constantius of Lyon, *The Life of St Germanus of Auxerre*, ed. and trans. Thomas Noble and Thomas Head, in *Soldiers of Christ: Saints' Lives from Late Antiquity and the Early Middle Ages*, Pennsylvania State University Press, 1994.

(6) Gildas, *On the destruction of Britain*, Ed. Hugh Williams, Honourable Society of Cymmrodorion, 1899.

(7) Bede, *The Ecclesiastical History of the English People*, ed. Judith McClure and Roger Collins, Oxford World Classics, 1999, p.26–27.

[8] Bede (Op. Cit., pp. 197 and 192).

[9] Geoffrey Hindley, *A Brief History of the Anglo-Saxons*, Constable & Robinson Ltd, 2006, pp. 53 and 118

[10] Bede (Op. Cit., p.78).

[11] *The Anglo-Saxon Chronicles*, trans. & collated Anne Savage, Book Club Associates,1983. Entries quoted are on pp. 29 and 35.

[12] Malcolm Todd, *Roman Britain*, Fontana Press, 1985, p.29 and map on p.31.

[13] John Morris, *The Age of Arthur*, Phoenix, 1973, p. 588.

[14] Miles Russell, *Roman Sussex*, 2006, chapters 2 – 5).

[15]Tacitus, Agricola , in *The Agricola and the Germania*, Penguin Classics, trans. H. Mattingly 1948, revised trans. S.A. Handford 1970, p.64.

[16] Bede (Op. Cit., much of pp.37 – 197].

[17] Bede (Op. Cit., p.192].

[18] Bede (Op. Cit., p.193)

[19] Bede (Op.Cit., pp. 193-4)

[20] Bede (Op. Cit., p. 130].

[21] Eddius Stephanus, *Life of Wilfrid*, in *The Age of Bede*, Penguin Classics, 1965 reprinted 2000, pp. 150–151.

[22] Eddius Stephanus (Op. Cit., p. 120 –122).

[23] E.V. Lucas, *Highways and Byways in Sussex*, Second edition 1935, reprinted 1950, frontispiece.

[24] E.V. Lucas, Op. Cit., pp.152-153.

[25] Henry Martin, *The History of Brighton and Environs*, John Beal, 1871.

[26] http://www.sussexpast.co.uk/property/site.php?site_id=13 as at 10.02.11.

[27] Paul Newman, *Lost Gods of Albion: The Chalk Hill Figures of Britain*, The History Press Ltd, 2009.

[28] *Eastbourne Gazette*, 29 April 1874 (Op. Cit. Newman, p.134).

[29] Newman (Op. Cit., p. 140).

[30] Newman (Op. Cit., p.144).

[31] Newman (Op. Cit., p.150).

[32] http://www.anderidagorsedd.org/Anderida_Gorsedd/Home.html as at 10.02.11.

[33] Based on the work of Walter Godfrey and Cecil Piper, ed. Frank Fox-Wilson, *A Guide to St. Andrew's Church Alfriston and the Church of the Good Shepherd Lullington*, as available February 2011.

[34] Based on Godfrey/Piper, Ed. Fox-Wilson (Op.Cit., p.16).

[35] Based on Godfrey/Piper, Ed. Fox-Wilson (Op.Cit., p.17).

[36] Geoffrey Hindley (Op. Cit., p.133).

[37] E.V. Lucas (Op. Cit., p.220).

[38] Rose Collis, *The New Encyclopaedia of Brighton*: Based on the original by Tim Carder, Brighton & Hove City Council, 2010, p.100.

[39] E.V. Lucas (Op.Cit., p.334).

[40] E.V. Lucas (Op.Cit., p.335).

[41] Tony Wales, *Sussex Ghosts and Legends*, Countryside Books, 1992, p. 31–32.

[42] Haxam Films, 1999.

[43] Joan Langhorne, *Holy Trinity Bosham*, PCC Holy Trinity Church, Bosham, 2006, p.1.

[44] Miles Russell (Op. Cit., pp. 110–112).

[45] Judith Glover, *The Place Names of Sussex*, B.T Batsford, 1975, Glossary on p.ix.

[46] Judith Glover (Op.Cit., pp. 83, 102 and 174).

[47] Judith Glover (Op. Cit., p.69)

[48] Joan Langhorne (Op. Cit., p. 17).

[49] Geoffrey W. Marwood, *The Stone Coffins of Bosham Church*, Penny Royal Publications, 2007, p.9.

[50] Geoffrey W. Marwood (Op. Cit., p. 4).

[51] Joan Langhorne (op. Cit., p.18).

[52] http://www.westsussex.info/bosham.shtml as at 25.02.11.

[53] *The Anglo-Saxon Chronicles*, (Op. Cit., pp. 164 – 167).

[54] Sir Frank Stenton, *Anglo-Saxon England*, Oxford History of England, Oxford University Press 1971, pp. 396 – 419.

[55] Alex Woolf, in *The Kings and Queens of England*, ed. W.M. Ormerod, Tempus Publishing Ltd, 2001, p.37.

[56] Joan Langhorne (Op. Cit., p.2)

[57] *The Chronicle of Battle Abbey*, ed. and trans. by Eleanor Searle, Oxford University Press, 1980, p.45.

[58] Guy, Bishop of Amiens, *Carmen de Hastingae Proelio* (The Song of the Battle of Hastings), ed. and trans. by Frank Barlow, Clarendon Press Oxford 1999, p.35.

[59] *The Waltham Chronicle*, ed. and trans. by L. Watkiss and M. Chibnall, Oxford Medieval Texts, 1994, pp. 46 – 56.

[60] Geoffrey M. Marwood (Op. Cit., p.6).

[61] John Pollock, *Harold: Rex Is King Harold buried in Bosham Church?* Penny Royal Publications 1996.

[62] Joan Langhorne (Op. Cit., p.2).

[63] Reader's Digest Association, *Folklore, Myths and Legends of Britain*, Reader's Digest Association Limited, 1973, p. 207.

[64] David Farmer, *Oxford Dictionary of Saints*, Oxford University Press, 4th edition 1997, pp. 303-304.

[65] Ed. F.L. Cross & E.A. Livingstone, *Oxford Dictionary of the Christian Church*, Oxford University Press, 3rd edition 1997, p. 970.

[66] Gen. ed. Elizabeth Hallam, *Saints*, Weidenfeld & Nicholson, London, 1994, p. 102.

[67] Revised Sarah Fawcett Thomas, *Butler's Lives of the Saints*, new full edition, Burnes and Oates, November volume, pp. 45–46.

[68] David Farmer (Op. Cit., p. 304).

[69] Edmund Cartwright, *The Parochial Topography of the Rape of Bramber in the Western Division of the County of Sussex*, J.B. Nicholls and Son, London, 1830, p.365.

[70] A.C. Crookshank, *St. Leonard of Sussex*, London: Arthur H. Stockwell, 1922.

[71] Hilaire Belloc, *The Four Men*, 1902, Tim Stacey Ltd 1971, pp.78–79.

[72] Pers. comm., 15.04.11.

[73] Sheila Kaye-Smith, *Weald of Kent and Sussex*, Robert Hale Limited, London, 1953, p.111.

[74] Edmund Cartwright (Op. Cit., pp. 365–366).

[75] E.V. Lucas (Op. Cit., p. 143–145).

[76] Sheila Kaye-Smith (op. Cit., p. 113–114).

[77] J. Mainwaring Baines, *Burton's St. Leonards*, Hastings Museum 1956, p.1.

[78] Baines (Op. Cit., p.11).

[79] Pers. comm., 09.03.11.

[80] W. V. Cooper, *A History of the Parish of Cuckfield*, C. Clarke, 1912, pp.118–119.

[81] W.V. Cooper, ibid., p. 121.

[82] http:/www.british-history.ac.uk/report.aspx?compid=56940

[83] Sir Bernard Burke CB LL.D., *The General Armory of England, Scotland, Ireland and Wales*, London: Harrison, 1884.

[84] Pers. comm., 23.03.11.

[85] J F. Huxford, *Arms of Sussex Families*, London & Chichester, Phillimore & Co. Ltd 1982, pp. 197–198.

[86] Pers. comm., 09.06.11.

[87] *St Margaret's Church, West Hoathly*, Sussex: Re-printed in 1976 for the Parochial Church Council.

[88] Peter Gaunt, *The English Civil Wars 1642–1651*, Osprey Publishing Ltd, 2003, p.23.

[89] Peter Gaunt (Op. Cit., p. 36.)

[90] Peter Gaunt (Op. Cit., pp. 38, 42, and 43)

[91] W.V. Cooper (Op. Cit., p. 203).

[92] J.R. Armstrong, *A History of Sussex*, Phillimore & Co. Ltd, 1961, 3rd edition 1974, reprinted 1978, p.107.

[93] Robin Milner-Gulland, article in Sussex Archeological Collections no. 126 (1988), 93–103, reprinted as *Welcome to Greatham Church: Brief Notes on the History and Construction of the Church*, as available at March 2011.

[94] E.V. Lucas (Op. Cit., p.157).

[95] Watney, Simon, *Bloomsbury in Sussex*, Alfriston, Sussex, Snake River Press 2007, pp. 6, 12, 36, 41, 10 and 7.

[96] Watney (Op. Cit., p.7).

[97] Watney (Op. Cit., p. 80).

[98] Watney (Op. Cit., p. 82).

[99] Watney (Op. Cit., pp. 86–87).

[100] Watney (Op. Cit., p.79).

[101] Watney (Op. Cit., p.84)

[102] Watney (Op. Cit., p.50)

[103] Watney (Op. Cit., p.49)

[104] Watney (Op. Cit., p.28)

[105] *St. Michael and All Angels, Berwick, East Sussex: A guide to the Church and 20th Century Bloomsbury Murals*, as available May 2011.